Just-Right Books for Beginning Readers

LEVELED BOOKLISTS & READING STRATEGIES

by
Ellen J. Brooks

SCHOLASTIC
PROFESSIONAL BOOKS

NEW YORK • TORONTO • LONDON • AUCKLAND • SYDNEY

For Rob

Cover design by Vincent Ceci and Jaime Lucero
Interior design by Solutions by Design, Inc.
Interior illustrations by James Graham Hale
Cover photo © Superstock.

ISBN 0-590-49243-8
12 11 10 9 8 7 6 5 4 3   8 9/9/01/0
Copyright © 1996 by Scholastic Inc. All rights reserved.

Printed in the U.S.A.

Table of Contents

ACKNOWLEDGMENTS

My love of books is an integral part of my work with young children in classrooms. My firm belief in both literature and children is deeply rooted in the past, beginning in my early childhood years, and continuing to my experiences as an adult. I would like to thank each of the following people for helping to shape my thinking on literacy, teaching, and learning:

My mother and father, who introduced literature into my life. As a child, my earliest memories are of my father reading to me each night at bedtime. The combination of love and undivided attention, along with a sense of freedom and choice (so rare at age three, at least from the child's point of view) mixed together to form an indelible image in my mind. In those read-aloud sessions, I learned the pleasures of story, and the routine of reading became a treasured part of the bedtime ritual.

My sixth-grade teacher, Mr. Lee Gray, who nurtured young writers and listened with care and interest to the stories of children. From him I learned to love writing, reading, and teaching.

My undergraduate adviser at the Pennsylvania State University and the director of the Treetop Nursery School in State College, Pennsylvania, Dr. David Butt, who kindled my fascination with children's talk and the process of language acquisition. It was Dave Butt who offered me my first teaching position. As a nursery-school teacher, I listened to three- and four-year-olds converse. There I was mesmerized by children's stories about real-life and imaginary experiences, transporting the players to a world far away—a world of dreams, make-believe, and magic. In that context, I learned the importance of carefully observing children, the power of make-believe, and the lure of literature.

Morton Botel, professor at the University of Pennsylvania, who offered me an alternative view of the development of literacy and the instructional process. Under his guidance, I gained a better understanding of the reading process and how children become readers and writers. The links between a holistic perspective and corresponding classroom practice opened up new possibilities for the children in my classroom. Mort also invited me into a community of learners, and the excitement and commitment to collaborative work that I experienced in graduate school has forever shaped my thinking, my teaching, and my relationships. I learned firsthand about the powerful effects of the social context on learning and literacy, and I reaped the rewards of personal and professional growth through this learning experience.

My friends and colleagues in the Mamaroneck Public Schools in Westchester County, New York, who have supported my work and helped me to learn, grow, and enjoy the pleasures of life in classrooms: Pat Fanning, Ruth Weiss, Mary Jane Feleppa, Jeannine Miller, Dolores Thompson, Janet LePre, Alice Dunning, Julie Walker, Nancy Bakerman, Nancy Stephens, Ronni Lee, Tracy Strub, Cathy Gabel, Donna Russell, Susan Rosenblum, Gail Boyle, Carol Dold, Trish Ellingwood, Madeline Longo, Maria Ellin, Roni Leibowitz, Barbara Mencher, Gloria Jordan, Ginger Stevenson, Judy Lesch, Ann Petrie, Peter Berendt, Joy Anastos, Teresa Silver, Susan Hurley, Susan Voina, Betsy Nolan, Barry Koski, Susan Herron, Susan Luther, Joanna Walsh, and Dr. Calvert E. Schlick, Jr.

Those friends who offered their moral support as well as their insights into the process of learning to read, both at home and at school: Ellen Biblowitz, Ann Chase, Laurie Freeman, Barbara Tessler, and Lisa Witten.

And finally, Terry Cooper at Scholastic Inc., and Susan Shafer, who asked important questions and helped me to rethink, refine, and document my experience in a way that would speak to teachers, parents, and other interested professionals.

Introduction

My experiences as a reader, a teacher, and a teacher-trainer have shaped my belief in the power of literature to motivate children to read.

I spend my days in classrooms, reading with children and collaborating with teachers to find ways to best support students' developing literacy. I am a reading specialist in the Mamaroneck public schools, where I work with teachers and students in two schools—the Central School, in Larchmont, New York, and Mamaroneck Avenue School, in Mamaroneck, New York. (My work is part of the Reading Support Program, which is an extension of the general classroom reading program. Unlike pullout programs, this program offers in-class support to young learners.) My goal is to find children's strengths and build on those to enhance children's learning. This means that I look for ways in which each child is distinct and work with the classroom teacher to formulate a plan to capitalize on that strength. For example, where one child loves to read a particular type of book (such as joke books), another will respond to writing or telling about a nonfiction story. Once we know that child's special area, we plan lessons and activities that create even greater interest and involvement.

In this book, you will read about a variety of children, from a child whose love of performing in plays led to a further interest in books to one who profited from reading with a friend. In these and other stories, you may find approaches that will work well with the children in your own class.

My work in the schools is balanced by my teaching at Manhattanville College, in Purchase, New York. As an adjunct assistant professor, I teach graduate reading courses, which also enhances my involvement with literature in the lives of children and adults alike. My work there confirms my belief in the need to encourage engagement and active response in all learners.

WITH YOU IN MIND

With this book my goal is to give teachers who are developing a literature-based program a place to start. My aim is to give teachers who have used, or are using, a literature-based program a range of techniques, ideas, and strategies for the classroom. The book is a guide for choosing and using children's literature to help youngsters develop as readers and writers. The text is intended for all teachers and parents interested in the role that literature can play in learning to read, and it is in no way limited to any single approach or method of instruction.

RECURRING THEMES

This book addresses three main topics: the power of literature in promoting literacy, criteria for selecting books for young readers, and ways to use books effectively with children.

Throughout, I emphasize that books have the potential to charm, delight, amuse, intrigue, and capture the reader. Like an adult, a child can be swept away by a good story, choosing to read that book many times over, sharing the book with a friend, and cherishing the experience. In this love of a single story, the seeds of literacy can flourish. The sheer pleasure of the book experience can pave the way to learning to read.

Readers of this book also will find considerable attention devoted to how to select books, including general guidelines and specific recommendations. The list of children's titles on pages 82–113 is comprehensive but not exhaustive. I've included it to illustrate how to build a classroom or home library. Also included are recommendations that will encourage the child's understanding of and active involvement in the reading process.

BOOK'S FORMAT

Chapter 1 explores the role of personal literacy, illustrating how our personal experiences guide us in making instructional decisions. It also outlines important conditions for encouraging young learners to soar in reading and writing.

Chapter 2 offers guidelines for selecting literature for emergent and beginning readers.

Chapter 3 offers suggestions for using literature to teach emergent and beginning readers.

Chapter 4 addresses the role of the teacher, describing how teachers can guide book selection and support the learning process.

Chapter 5 includes ideas for working with parents and includes many actual handouts that you can use, and that we sent to parents of our students.

Chapter 6 includes sample case studies that demonstrate the valuable role that literature can play in learning to read.

Chapter 7 describes general stages of reading development and lists good books for a beginning reading program. For your convenience, it is organized by genre, and by author, title, and level.

LEARNERS ALL

Teaching reading is an active process, one that requires continual reflecting and refining until it encompasses a knowledge about the reading process, about children's literature, about individual children, and about the classroom as a community of learners. Writing this book has helped me to refine my own thoughts on the teaching and learning process. It has been a source of inspiration for my work in the classroom and caused me to rethink my own practice. I hope that the text is enjoyable and easy for you to read, and that it will inspire and inform the methods you use to teach children to read.

CHAPTER 1

Encouraging Children's Reading Independence Through Good Books

Overview

I have found that teaching is a very personal process. Just as children bring past experiences, resources, and their own view of the world to bear on classroom life, teachers—you and I— bring personal experiences to classroom work as well. I've discovered that by examining the early experiences that taught me to love reading, and to teach others to read, I can identify the principles that guide my professional practices and decision making today. I invite you to do the same.

I begin this chapter by describing some childhood experiences that contributed to my early interest in reading. I also explain how I learned later, as an adult, to teach others to teach and read. On pages 13–15, I outline some basic conditions for encouraging children to read and write. These are based on my own observations and my reading of the works of educational researchers.

Personal Literacy and the Teaching Process

It was in graduate school that I first began the process of examining my own early literacy experiences. In course work with Morton Botel at the University of Pennsylvania, colleagues and I reflected on early experiences in learning to read and on positive experiences with significant adults in our childhoods.

I remember my delight as a child, for example, when my father read to me each night at bedtime. I was always given the option of choosing the story, even if it meant Dad had to read aloud the same story many evenings in a row. Other important reading experiences that come to mind include reading great books to myself under the covers with a flashlight, getting my first library card, and rereading favorite books, such as *The Cat in the Hat*, the Little Golden Books, and the *Nancy Drew* mystery series.

Many years after my course with Dr. Botel, I read Donald Graves's *Discover Your Own Literacy* (Heinemann, 1990). That book helped me to understand the role of personal literacy and the reflective process. Graves provided me with both the language for articulating the importance of this process and the tools for sharing this dimension of classroom life with my graduate students at Manhattanville College in Purchase, New York.

In his writing, Graves talks about the value of listening to and observing students. Through his work and that of Pat Carini and Denny Taylor, among others, I have learned new ways to continue the ongoing process of discovering my own personal literacy and sharing it with others.

Perhaps you too can think back to some positive experiences in your youth in which reading gave you pleasure, and to the adults who encouraged you. Then explore how to duplicate in some way those happy experiences for the youngsters in your own classroom. These may be sessions in which you read aloud to your class, introducing well-chosen books and providing children with time to read and enjoy pictures on their own.

Son Teaches Mom a Lesson

What is the key image that comes to mind when I think of my past experiences? The power of literature. One important incident with my son stands out. It shows that reading a book can be a powerful experience. It also makes clear that the child is at the center of the learning process.

When Rob entered first grade, he was beginning to read some easy, predictable books with a minimal amount of support, but he was not at all forthcoming about reading aloud at home. I remember once, early in the school year, I was reading a book to him. He was quietly attempting to read some of the words himself as he followed along. Quite pleased to see this interest, and curious to hear him read more, I suggested that he take a turn. He became indignant. "*You* read the book," he insisted. Quickly, he put me in my place, for, of course, I was the mother—it was my role to read *to* him. I reminded myself how important it was not to slip into the teacher role, but rather, to continue, as a parent, to nurture and support his development. I also recognized that his response revealed something about Rob that we have seen with many new learning experiences. He likes to practice and rehearse on his own; when he feels confident in his newly acquired ability, he will allow others to observe. Rob hangs back until he is sure of himself. At least at home, reading was not going to be any different.

I settled into my "mother" role, reading to Rob and bringing home interesting books to share as often as I could. One day, in the late fall, I brought home a book of jokes—*Ten Copycats in a Boat and Other Riddles* by Alvin Schwartz, part of the *I Can Read* series (HarperCollins, 1980). I read the jokes to Rob and his friend, and they had a wonderful time laughing and guessing the

11

punch lines. The boys asked for more. I read the book to them again, their delight even more apparent the second time through. Later that evening, as I was cooking dinner, Rob was busy reading the book. Every now and then, he would come over to ask me to read a word for him.

Child + Good Book + Teacher = Success

The next day, anxious to share the jokes with his friends, Rob took the book to school. His teacher was quick to see the possibilities in the situation and invited him to share the book with the class at circle time. Rob's enthusiasm wiped out any sense of self-consciousness he might ordinarily have. The jokes were clearly "the thing"—reading merely served the purpose of sharing this pleasure with the other children.

"When is a car not a car?" asked Rob. "When it turns into a parking lot," he answered. The book became the hottest reading material in the classroom. Soon Rob and his friends began to make their own joke books. The classroom buzzed with activity, some children copying the jokes from the book, others inventing their own.

My small purchase at a school book fair turned out to be a priceless investment for Rob and his classmates. The book offered many hooks and ways into literacy. Rob loved the jokes, savoring each one over and over with his friends and on his own. The text itself promoted independence by allowing him to use a variety of strategies for reading, including picture clues, sentence context, and overall meaning. After listening to the jokes read to him, he could draw on his memory of them when he read the book on his own. Rob had a sense of personal satisfaction that he was "doing it on his own." In school, his confidence was boosted even more when he shared the jokes with the class. From that point on, he seemed to think of himself as a reader, and he was willing to read aloud, regardless of the audience—even to his parents. The key was his interest in sharing a particular book, and if the interest was there, he was willing to read.

The joke book also brought together a community of learners in Rob's classroom. His teacher, recognizing the children's enthusiasm for the book, allowed the jokes to take center stage for almost three weeks. She nurtured the children's interest and facilitated the writing of their own versions of the book.

From this experience I was once again reminded of the power of the book in forming an effective literature-based reading program.

Foundation for Learning

What are some important conditions for encouraging children to read and write? I outline some below, many based on the work of notable researchers in the field. These conditions apply to all children—those for whom learning to read is a struggle and those who learn to read naturally, with little adult guidance or direct instruction.

* Children learn to read and write by engaging in meaningful, purposeful reading and writing activities. Instruction is most effective when it is in response to a child's need to know. Learning begins with the child and those resources the child brings to the learning context. (Kenneth Goodman, *What's Whole in Whole Language?* Portsmouth, NH: Heinemann, 1986.)

* Children learn to read by reading, by seeing the whole, not by learning a series of discrete subskills. The ideal classroom supports the holistic nature of reading and writing and keeps language whole and meaningful.

    One of our first tasks as teachers is to have children "get" the big picture, to understand the communicative purposes of reading and writing, and to recognize that there are many strategies for reading. (Goodman)

* Children learn through their interactions with books, and with each other, and through discussion and active involvement. The social context is an important variable for learning literacy, and the classroom must promote social interaction and student collaboration. Learning is both social and personal. We all learn from direct, interactive experience.

    Books can also be a powerful influence in bringing people—children, teachers, and parents— together. (Marilyn Cochran-Smith, *The Making of a Reader*, Norwood, NJ: Ablex, 1984. Shirley Brice Heath, *Ways with Words: Language, Life and Work in Communities and Classrooms*, London: Cambridge University Press, 1983.)

* Children move toward independence in reading and writing through involvement in decision making. They need opportunities to choose their own books and to experience a variety of response options in the

classroom, from talking to writing, drawing, and dramatizing.

Involving students in goal setting ("I want to read three chapter books this month") and in the assessment process ("I still can't figure out books with lots of characters") is an important part of decision making. By providing options, choices, and opportunities for children, teachers foster personal investment and a sense in children that they can have a role in directing the course of their own learning. (Patricia Carini, "Another Way of Looking," *Education and Democracy*, ed. K. Jervis and A. Tobier, Weston, MA: The Cambridge School, 1988.)

* Children learn to read and write by having working models. Regie Routman uses the term *demonstrations* to describe the importance to children of observing the process of reading and of writing in action. She says that the models need not be perfect. Rather, students learn by listening to teachers think out loud and make mistakes. All children need models; they are a powerful source of learning.

  Children also need time for practice, without the constraints that often appear when practice is observed by a teacher or adult. Children learn by rehearsing in private. They work things through in their own way. (Brian Cambourne, *The Whole Story: Natural Learning and the Acquisition of Literacy in the Classroom*, Richmond Hill, Ontario, Canada: Scholastic-TAB Publications Ltd., 1988. Don Holdaway, *The Foundations of Literacy*, New York: Ashton Scholastic, 1979. Regie Routman, *Invitations: Changing as Teachers and Learners K-12*, Portsmouth, NH: Heinemann, 1991.)

* Children learn to read and write through active exploration and play with language, and through a wide variety of general experiences. Through this immersion in literate activity, children begin to form their own hypotheses regarding the printed word. The ideal classroom is one in which children are learning by doing and actively exploring language: Books are readily available and there is time to become immersed in them. (Cambourne, Holdaway)

* Children learn best in an atmosphere where they feel free to take risks, and where they can learn through trial and error, through their mistakes. The importance of trial and error is parallel to the process of language acquisition, in which the role of successive approximations is key to development. (An example is when a one-year-old imitates a

parent's words, saying, for example "dada" for *daddy*.)

✳ Reading and writing are language-based processes and part of the communication arts, along with listening and speaking. (Morton Botel and Susan Lytle, *The Pennsylvania Comprehensive Reading and Communication Arts Plan* II [*PCRP II*], Harrisburg, PA: Pennsylvania Department of Education, 1988.) Teachers should recognize the interrelationship of the communication arts and the strong connections between learning to talk and learning to read.

✳ There are multiple entry points into literacy. The ideal classroom accommodates children's individual differences. Good teachers recognize the importance of finding the "hooks" for each child. The role of the arts is primary for many children. (Hoyt, L., "Many Ways of Knowing: Using Drama, Oral Interactions, and the Visual Arts to Enhance Reading Comprehension," *The Reading Teacher*, April 1992.)

✳ Children are best supported in their learning by teachers who observe their students carefully, reflect on those observations, and use their knowledge of what children *can* do to support their learning. This is achieved through systematic observation and recording of these observations. This process, in turn, promotes our own professional growth and allows us to reflect on and refine our own teaching practice.

✳ We must recognize and use children's *strengths and interests* to facilitate their growth.

The developmental process is often very different for each child. For some, it may be a particular book that provides the hook; for others, the writing on a cereal box the child sees each morning at breakfast. For still others, the path to reading may be found through writing.

Since good books are so important to literacy, it makes sense to ask, "What guidelines can we use for choosing books, for immersing children in the world of literature?" You'll find some answers to that question in the next chapter.

CHAPTER 2

How to Choose Books for Emergent and Beginning Readers

In my talks with teachers over the years, I have noticed a marked increase in interest in children's books. More than ever before, many teachers want to find out which exciting children's books are newly published, which books will appeal to children at a particular grade level, and which tie in well with specific social-studies or science units. In workshops I give or attend, I've found that the topic of children's literature often binds teachers together. It highlights our shared vision for developing readers, writers, and literate thinkers of our students.

As teachers, we want to encourage a love of literature and reading, always looking for material that will hook kids on books. This chapter focuses on how to choose books that will support beginning reading instruction. The chapter also outlines a set of criteria that provides the basis for selecting good books; it guides in the creation of a diverse and balanced literature collection.

Ah, My Favorite!

Choose books that kids will love, books that amuse, intrigue, and delight young readers. That's what children's author Margaret Mahy said in a speech at a convention of teachers (IRA, San Antonio, April 1993). She says that "real stories" make sense to kids. These books give kids pleasure in learning to read and in gaining ideas of the world. "Real stories" allow children to get enjoyment from reading and to learn to read at the same time.

I have learned to choose books that *I* want to read with children, books that I hope they will want to reread and take home to share with a friend or their family. When I choose such books, that excitement is readily apparent to children. I know it's quite contagious. What else is important?

From Animal Stories to Mysteries, Easy to Challenging

I've learned the importance of having a rich and varied literature collection in the classroom. With books of many types, from poetry to fantasy, children become exposed to the complexity of literature, offering them many options. You, the teacher, play an important role in expanding children's knowledge of good literature. Through sharing and reading aloud, you can expose children to great books of various levels, styles, and genres.

First, it is important to stock your classroom library with books of different levels, including challenging books, comfortable books, and "easy" books. Easy books allow the beginning reader to feel successful, to have the experience of "fluent reading " with a book that is effortless to read.

Other titles in the classroom collection can offer more challenging experiences, in which the child selects a book and reads with the teacher. Fielding and Roller (1992) recommend supporting the reading of difficult books through reading aloud to children, partner reading, and rereading. "Making easy books acceptable" can be achieved through modeling and sharing or through changing the purpose for reading (for example, suggesting that a second-grade child practice a book to read to a younger sibling or a first-grader in the school).

Planning for diversity of genre is another key dimension of variety. We want to expose children to many different types of books for many reasons, not the least of which is that children have individual preferences and interests. One child might gravitate toward nonfiction, based on specific topics of interest ("I'm a fan of books about the presidents"). Another child might love reading and writing poetry ("Shel Silverstein makes me laugh"). A good classroom library will have books that appeal to children with widely diverse interests.

Predictable Books

Goldilocks and the Three Bears. Henny Penny. Brown Bear, Brown Bear, What Do You See? Predictable books such as these—with rhyme, rhythm, repetition, or a common story pattern—help young learners read. Here's why.

READING IS A STRATEGIC PROCESS

In the early stages of learning to read, the child experiments with print, using context and prior knowledge to tackle unfamiliar words. The more children learn to read, the more they employ a range of strategies, including using picture clues, guessing based on overall meaning, thinking about what might make sense in the sentence, and attacking the word through knowledge of word analysis. In this sense, "strategies" refers to the child's developing ability to make meaning, to make predictions, to figure out a new or unknown word, and to take a guess based on available cues in the text and the child's own prior knowledge.

The child's transition through the early stages of learning to read and the acquisition of strategies for reading can be facilitated by certain features of the text. These features provide useful guidelines for selecting books for a classroom library and for making choices for individual children.

Choosing stories that are familiar to children is one way we can facilitate the child's use of strategies. With familiar stories (for example, fairy tales or folktales that the child has heard before), the child has a set of expectations that allow for predicting events or phrases based on prior knowledge of the plot. For example, many children enjoy easy-to-read versions of familiar fairy tales, even though the actual text may be very limited and lacking in richness and detail. However, the plot is already familiar, and children can fill in the gaps on their own because the story is so well known. (They can tell ahead of time, for example, that in *The Three Little Pigs* the wolf will try to blow down the house of the third pig.) For this reason, the reading experience can be successful. Consider stocking your classroom library with a range of predictable books.

OTHER CRITERIA

There are several other features that contribute to the predictability of a text:

* Rhyme

* Rhythmic language

* Repetitive structures (for example, repetition of words or phrases, and repetition of story structure)

* Common story patterns

Some books with predictable text structures include:

* *Brown Bear, Brown Bear, What Did You See?* by Bill Martin, Jr.

* *Dear Zoo* by Rod Campbell

* *Down by the Bay* by Raffi

* *Hattie and the Fox* by Mem Fox

* *Greedy Cat,* by Joy Cowley

* *If You Give a Mouse a Cookie* by Laura Numeroff

* *Is Your Mama a Llama?* by Deborah Guarino

* *It Looked Like Spilt Milk* by Charles G. Shaw

* *The Hungry Caterpillar* by Eric Carle

* *Three Aesop Fox Fables* by Paul Galdone

Appealing Illustrations That Support the Text

For many of us, whether adult or child, illustrations often capture our attention and draw us to a particular book. Illustrations appeal to our aesthetic sense and have the potential to spark delight and intrigue, involving us with the reading experience in powerful ways. Who would not be drawn to Sucie Stevenson's humorous illustrations in *Henry and Mudge*, or Bruce Degen's pictures in *Jamberry*?

Illustrations that closely follow the text and allow the child to follow the story also offer another way to predict the text. Detailed pictures, such as those in Ann Rockwell's nonfiction books, often provide cues that the child can use with ease. Illustrations play an important role in conveying the story and the overall mood and tone, offering the reader a rich source of information to weave together with the text. Frequently, when a child is just beginning to read independently, the picture clues allow

Example of books with appealing illustrations that support the text include:

* *Arthur* series, written and illustrated by Marc Brown

* *Fishing* and *Gino Badino* by Diana Engel

* *Henry and Mudge* series by Cynthia Rylant, illustrated by Sucie Stevenson

* *Hooray for Snail!* by John Stadler

* *Mitchell Is Moving* by Marjorie Weinman, illustrated by Jose Aruego

* *Tales of Oliver Pig* by Jean Van Leeuwen, illustrated by Arnold Lobel

for a reading that captures the meaning, even though the child may make substitutions for some of the actual words. When choosing books for your students, then, think about books with pictures that will draw them in.

Inviting Laughter and Active Involvement

Humorous books are very appealing to young children; these books seem to hook more children than any other genre. Children frequently select collections of jokes, riddles, puns, and other forms of speech play, as well as humorous poems. Because of the universal appeal of humor, these books have great potential for supporting beginning readers. The books invite shared reading, rereading, and other follow-up activities.

In one first-grade classroom that I visit, reading and writing humorous poems became a routine for the children in the class. Inspired by a whole-class read-aloud experience with Jack Prelutsky's poems, the children asked if they could write funny poems of their own. This they did, and one poem led to another. Soon everyone in the class was busy crafting a poem. Over time, the collection grew, and the children put their work into a book for the classroom library. The intrigue and enjoyment of humor resulted in a literature activity

IRRESISTIBLE BOOKS

Children will enjoy the zany poetry of Shel Silverstein and Jack Prelutsky, the wacky adventures of Peggy Parish's *Amelia Bedelia*, and the silly humor in Dr. Seuss's *The Cat in the Hat* or Rita Golden Gelman's *More Spaghetti I Say*. The range of possibilities in this area is tremendous. Other favorites include:

* *Fox All Week,* and other *Fox* books by Edward Marshall
* *Frog and Toad* by Arnold Lobel
* *Grizzly Riddles* by Katy Hall and Lisa Eisenberg
* *I Saw You in the Bathtub and Other Folk Rhymes* by Alvin Schwartz
* *Leo, Zack, and Emmie* by Amy Ehrlich
* *Mrs. Brice's Mice* by Syd Hoff
* *Old Turtle's Soccer Team,* and others by Leonard Kessler
* *Three by the Sea* by Edward Marshall

that for weeks of the school year supported these developing readers and writers in many ways.

Does the Book Celebrate Language?

Each time I read a book that I'm wild about, I find myself wrapped up in the story *and* in the way the author has chosen to use words to propel the story. In the classroom, when we share books with children, we have an opportunity to show literature as a celebration of language and to focus children's attention on how different authors use language. By reading aloud and through discussions of literature, we can help children to recognize and appreciate the joys of language.

Mem Fox, in *Radical Reflections* (1993), describes this process from her perspective as an author, citing her aim constantly to choose the right words, to use words in a way that will make the reading experience take on a life of its own. She says, "I try to write rhythmically and repetitively to ensure that my words dance inside the child's head long after the story is finished" (p. 138).

There are so many well-written books, and much depends on personal preference. Some of my favorites include books by Arthur Dorros (*Abuela*), Mem Fox (*Hattie and the Fox; Koalu Lou*), Arnold Lobel (*The Book of Pigericks*), Bill Martin, Jr. and John Archambault (*Knots on a Counting Rope*), Patricia Polacco (*Thunder Cake* and *Mrs. Katz and Tush*), William Steig (*Brave Irene; Sylvester and the Magic Pebble*), and Jane Yolen (*Owl Moon*).

CHAPTER 3

Using Literature to Teach Emergent and Beginning Readers

One Story, Many Learners

In a quiet corner of the first-grade classroom, six-year-old Sara was poring over *Greedy Cat* by Joy Cowley. Mrs. B., who had read the big-book version to the whole class the day before, walked over to Sara and invited her to read the book aloud. "Sure," responded Sara. Sara enjoyed the story about an adventurous pet who noses around the grocery bags each day, scouting for the next delicious treat. At the end of the story, Mum realizes what's been going on, and leaves—no, not a tasty morsel, but—some pepper in the bag.

Sara seemed to read the story with ease and fluency. She used her finger to keep track of the words, and several times she hesitated, waiting for help. Overall, Mrs. B. noted the positive impact of several readings of the text, as Sara is a beginning reader who quickly caught on to the predictable nature of the story.

By the time Sara finished reading, there were three other children listening over her shoulder. At one point, the classmates helped identify the word *pepper*.

When the story was over, Mrs. B. asked, "What else do you think the woman might bring home from the store?" There was instant chatter; the children volunteered a range of ideas, from pizza to apples to vinegar.

Seeing the enthusiasm, Mrs. B. suggested that the children create their own version of *Greedy Cat*, using the basic story structure as guide. The project took several days to complete. Mrs. B. took dictation from the group, typed up the group story in book form, and had each child illustrate a personal copy of the book. When the children completed their books, Mrs. B. met with them as a group. The children read aloud from their individual, personalized copies of the tale.

This example combines several important teaching activities, including reading aloud, rereading to build fluency and confidence, and writing one's own version of a familiar story.

In this chapter, I offer a rationale for reading aloud to children as well as practical suggestions for doing so. The goal of the activities is to encourage children to be involved with books, to give an active response, and to help kids develop a range of reading strategies.

Reading Aloud: The Core Experience

Reading aloud has long been heralded as the single most potent factor in creating a love of story and of reading. When a teacher, parent, other adult, or older child reads aloud, the child's growth toward independent reading is encouraged.

Several specific benefits are most striking:

* Reading aloud provides a fertile context for emerging literacy. The value of reading aloud shows up in many areas, including the development of vocabulary (Ninio, A., and Bruner, J., 1973), the development of sense of story, book-handling skills, and early concepts of print (Huck, C. S., 1992).

* Reading aloud offers the child a model or demonstration of fluent reading. A child will hear the story and will develop an ear for the sound of a story read aloud, for the flow of oral language in story form.

* Reading aloud allows the child to preview a particular book. The child can gain a sense of the story, and this preview will facilitate the child's own rereading of the tale.

A Personal Tale

Very often, children choose books to read that they have heard before. My son came home one day with a book from the school library, *Gino Badino*, by Diane Engel. He was excited to share it with me and anxious to describe his experience listening as the school librarian read it aloud to the class. The second reading at home was a pleasurable and satisfying experience, although he did describe the first time as "more exciting because you don't know what is going to happen next, but the second time is just as good...in a different way." This knowledge of the story allows the child to develop a set of expectations, thus facilitating the rereading and offering a sense of satisfaction and self-confidence.

* Reading aloud offers a way to share books, to share a range of genre and authors, and to expand the child's knowledge of the universe of literature. Through reading many different types of books aloud, the teacher can also share the range of complexity of literature and dispel

the myth that "sophistication " in literature is related to the number of words on a page or the level of difficulty of the vocabulary. Reading aloud also provides a context for helping children to make connections, to experience different books focusing on the same theme or several books by the same author (Hoffman, J., et.al., 1993).

✳ Reading aloud, whether in a large group, small group, or with an individual child, provides a context for interaction about books. The shared experience binds people together, creating opportunities for developing literacy within a social context.

Rereading

Each semester, when I begin teaching a graduate course on reading/language arts instruction in the elementary school, I ask my students to write about the five books that had the most lasting influence on them and to describe the nature of that impact and why their choices are significant. It's an exercise that has great appeal for almost everyone. Invariably, there are many students who talk about reading a particular book several times, with each reading offering a different experience.

Rereading literature is like viewing a sculpture: Each time there is something new to see—a new perspective, a different interpretation, a richer understanding—and a more intimate personal connection with the work itself.

Children often choose the same book over and over, treasuring the familiarity of the experience and enjoying the intimacy of rereading a favorite story several times through. Rereading is a powerful vehicle for promoting literacy and love of story.

Rereading is also a powerful support for developing greater fluency and independence. Rereading a story provides rehearsal and practice. For many children, it is not until that second reading that they begin to put all the pieces together and actually "sound" like a reader. In this way, the beginning reader gains that inner sense of what it "feels" like to be a reader. According to Peter Johnston, an educator who conducted a workshop at Central School in Mamaroneck, New York, the experience is invaluable in the making of a reader.

Activities to Develop Strategies for Emerging Readers

Several gamelike activities offer a way for emerging readers to develop basic strategies (for example, word-by-word matching) and to be exposed to a core of basic books.

I sometimes adapt these "read aloud" games or activities for the more advanced readers, but they are particularly useful for the early readers. You can play them with the whole class, with a small group, or with individuals.

ECHO READING

Echo reading involves reading a line of text or a page of text to the child, and the child "echoes back" the text. Echo reading is an excellent technique for introducing a new book or giving a child the sense of what it feels like to read fluently.

Echo reading is also excellent for reading poetry because the technique encourages children to learn a poem by heart. Once a story or poem is committed to memory, this knowledge can be used to reread the text, teaching the child to develop the concept of word-by-word matching and building a sight vocabulary at the same time.

EXAMPLE:

Teacher (*reading aloud*): . . . not by the hair of my chinny, chin-chin.

Children: not by the hair of my chinny, chin-chin.

PREVIEWING THE TEXT

Previewing the book before reading increases overall success for many children, who enjoy discussing the title of the story, paging through the book, and becoming familiar with the illustrations. When you ask children to preview a book, you are asking them to develop an overall orientation and set of expectations about the story.

Previewing can take on various forms, from a brief discussion of the title and cover illustration to a more detailed "walk-through" of each page, engaging the child in describing and telling the story through the illustrations.

EXAMPLE:

Teacher: Look at the cover of the book. What do you see there?

Child: Well, there's a frog and a toad with clothes on. They're walking down a road.

RETELLING THE STORY

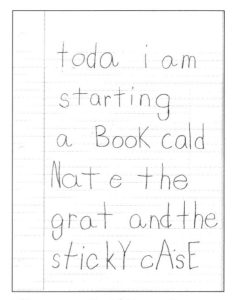

Retelling the story is an excellent technique for building under-standing and sense of story. The retelling allows the child to gain greater control of the story line.

EXAMPLE:

> *Child:* A big bad wolf shows up at the village where the three pigs live. He says to the first pig, "Let me in or I'll blow down your house."

Providing Options for Responding to Literature

When we give children opportunities to respond to literature, we offer them time to make personal connections with books, to extend their thinking and interaction with literature, to deepen and enrich the reading experience.

Response to literature can take on many different forms: writing, talking, drawing, role-playing, and other expressive venues.

EXAMPLES:

* Writing a new ending to the story
* Talking about what the child would have done if he or she were a character in the book
* Drawing a picture of a favorite scene
* Making up and singing a song about the story
* Performing a skit based on the story

READING RESPONSE JOURNALS

No matter the age of the read-er—from a six-year-old to an adult— response journals invite the reader to extend his or her thinking about a book, to stretch the response, and to examine an idea or concept carefully and closely. Gen-erally, responses are written but can also be expressed through drawing.

toda i am
starting
a Book cald
Nat e the
grat and the
stickY cAsE

Eli, age 7, writes his reaction to books in his response journal.

WRITING: REINVENTING A FAMILIAR STORY

Linking a reading experience with a follow-up writing activity has many benefits. Using the book as a springboard for writing allows for an extended experience that can support the growth of literacy and the child's investment in reading, writing, and literature.

You can adapt this for children at various stages of development. Among emerging readers, have a child or group of children dictate the story to you. As children develop greater fluency and control over print, they may begin to write their own stories with less support from you. You, a paraprofessional, or the children themselves can type the stories. The children can then illustrate them for a book.

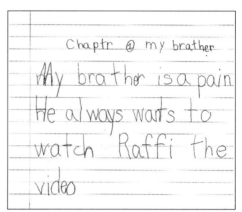

This child wrote a draft of his version of Judy Blume's *The Pain and the Great One*.

You may also want children to reinvent a familiar story, then use the new version as a book for reading.

LITERATURE DISCUSSIONS

Literature discussions offer another way of engaging your children in response to literature. You can lead such talks in a variety of formats, including large-group, small-group (such as that of a book club, which is often led by the students, with the teacher circulating from group to group), and teacher-to-student.

Through these opportunities you can encourage children's interest in the pleasures of reading and sharing responses to books.

EXAMPLE:

Teacher: Why do you think Little Red Riding Hood wasn't afraid to walk through the woods?

Child: Well, maybe she had taken that route lots of times. And nothing bad ever happened to her before.

Teacher: How would you have felt if you had met the wolf?

Child: At first, I wouldn't have been scared either. He didn't look so bad.

Teacher: What do you think of this story?

Child: I like it because the bad wolf got punished.

RESPONDING THROUGH THE ARTS

The arts offer many rich and varied opportunities for engaging children in responding to literature. The motivation to respond through the arts often emerges quite naturally, as the arts allow for reflecting on an experience with literature in a personal way.

The arts encourage active involvement and individual exploration of a text. Through drama, the visual arts (drawing, painting, photography, sculpture, and so forth), dance, and music, children can make connections with texts and reflect on their reading experience.

Possible Projects

* Create a puppet of a favorite character in a story, and put on plays and skits about the story.

* Stage a play of a favorite read aloud story or familiar fairy tale, giving the children the time and materials to create props, scenery, and costumes, and perhaps to write an invitation to other classes.

* Create a collage to describe a favorite character in the story, using cutouts from magazines.

* Ask children to draw, paint, or work with clay to express their personal response to the story or to depict a favorite character or part of the story.

* Design a new book jacket.

* Using movement and pantomime, act out a familiar story or scene from the story.

* Create a class mural as a response to a story.

* Reinvent a favorite story. After the children write their own version, they can publish it in book form.

Using the Shared Reading Experience to Extend Skills into Strategies

OVERVIEW

Literature-based instruction always seems to raise questions about how and if skills such as phonics, vocabulary, and comprehension are taught. An exchange I recently observed will illustrate the way in which one teacher incorporated skill teaching within a literature-based reading lesson:

At quiet reading time, Richard chooses B. Wiseman's *Morris the Moose* to read with his teacher. Together, student and teacher preview the book, discussing the title and several of the illustrations. Richard reads several pages with ease and fluency, displaying interest in the story and taking pleasure in his competence.

He continues: "'You have four legs and a tail and things on your hair [the text actually reads 'head'], said Morris.'" Mrs. S. pauses, drawing Richard's attention back to the word *head*. Covering the last letter of the word, she turns to him and says, "If this were *hair*, what would you expect to see at the end of the word?" Richard quickly catches on and realizes that the correct response is "head." Mrs. S. acknowledges that Richard's initial response did not significantly interfere with the meaning, but at the same time it is important to check yourself, to self-monitor your own reading. In this way, Mrs. S. prompts Richard and guides him through the reading process.

SKILLS OR STRATEGIES?

Routman (1991) distinguishes between skills and strategies, defining strategies as the ability to apply knowledge of skills within the context of a meaningful reading experience. "A skill," says Routman, "no matter how well it has been taught—cannot be considered a strategy until the learner can use it purposefully and independently...The learner must know how and when to apply the skill; that is what elevates the skill to the strategy level" (p. 135).

Fluent readers employ a variety of strategies for reading, with the goal of constructing meaning always primary. As children learn to read, they employ a range of strategies, including using picture clues, guessing based on overall meaning, and thinking about what might make sense in the sentence. Fluent readers use strategies automatically, without thinking. When children are learning to read, their efforts to read are often more deliberate, and strategies for reading are used at a more conscious level. Beginning reading programs guide children in developing a range of strategies for reading, and, while many will develop these strategies quite naturally, others require more direct, explicit instruction.

STRATEGIES BUILD BETTER READERS

Here are some strategies you can teach or model for your youngsters.

Picture Clues

Show children that the picture on the cover of a book gives clues about the story. Example: When reading, a child has difficulty with the word *spaceship*. Draw the child's attention to the beginning sound and mention that the picture offers cues for figuring out the word.

Try this: Before reading a story to the class, show the cover. Talk about what the children see there. What do children think the book will be about? After the story has been read, take another look at the cover. Were children's predictions about the book correct?

Title of Book

Discuss the title of the book and point out that the title often gives clues about the story. Hold up several books, from *Looking at Space* to *The Big Pumpkin*. Talk about what children are likely to find inside.

Relate Subject to Prior Knowledge

Help children realize that they already know things about the subject of a story and they can think about those things as they read. For example, before reading aloud a book entitled *Tales Mummies Tell*, children can make a list of things they already know about Egyptian mummies.

Make a Mental Picture

Ask children to picture a story in their minds. Point out that this will help them "see" the action and remember it more clearly. As you read aloud *Millions of Cats*, for example, have children close their eyes and visualize what the old man is doing at certain times.

Think What Will Occur Next

Remind children that they can make predictions about what will happen next in a story. Making predictions will make the story more interesting for them. As you read aloud *Doctor DeSoto*, pause in the middle and ask children what they think will happen next. Ask students to explain their answers.

Try Various Ways

Make children aware that when they come to a word they don't know in a story, they should try to figure it out. They can sound it out, guess the meaning through its context in the sentence, or reread the page to see what makes sense.

Fluent readers combine a range of strategies drawing upon a variety of skills. These skills include awareness of conventions (print and phonology), knowledge of sounds (phonology), relationships between letters and sounds (phonics), and knowledge of grammatical structures (syntax).

In addition to direct instruction, one particularly effective way to help children develop these skills is to provide time for them to practice what they know by playing games: those made commercially and those that are hand-made or improvised. Games such as those described below allow children to expand their knowledge of words, sentences, and longer passages. Try these:

WORD-MAKING GAMES

Be sure to stock one of your learning centers with board games including Boggle™, Scrabble™, MatchMe, and Concentration. The games can be played during independent activity time. As children play, they reinforce their knowledge of phonics, linguistic patterns, and structural analysis, though to them, the games only spell F-U-N.

SENTENCE-MAKING GAMES

Sentence-making activities provide additional practice in word recognition and sentence construction. Sentence making involves creating sentences from individual word cards. The complexity and number of words can be adapted to the individual needs of the child.

Be sure to use words from the child's own writing and/or from the reading selection. Your children will be actively engaged in the manipulation of the cards as they construct their own sentences. Sentence-making games encourage the child to combine knowledge about the detail of the word with meaning and context clues, thus encouraging the integration of strategies for reading.

EXPLORING SOUND-SYMBOL CONNECTIONS THROUGH POETRY AND SPEECH PLAY

Do you remember how much fun you and your friends had as young-sters when you recited the silly *Susan sells seashells by the sea-shore*? You can encourage your students to enjoy the sounds of language by introducing them to tongue twisters, poetry, and various forms of speech play. They are lively and engaging ways to build knowledge of language patterns. You can also organize choral-reading sessions and group recitations of favorite poems, those written by both the students and professionals. Who knows? You might find your students entering the lunchroom one day chanting *Peter Piper picked a peck of pickled peppers . . .*

CHAPTER 4

The Teacher's Role in a Literature-Based Classroom

Overview

The teachers I know have the ability to observe children carefully and tailor instruction to meet students' needs. They work toward extending children's learning and expanding youngsters' curiosity and imagination. These effective teachers guide children's book selection and scaffold the instructional experience to promote success.

In this chapter, I discuss these topics and offer some suggestions for classroom practice.

1. Guiding Book Selection

When you walk into a classroom in which literature is the center of the reading program, you are likely to see children scattered about the room with books in hand, perhaps sprawled across the floor or relaxing comfortably in a chair. Students might be reading with a friend or alone, and the teacher may well be reading with an individual child or a group in a corner of the room.

It takes time to register all the visual information. At first glance, it may even be difficult to identify the teacher. (She may be seated in a child's chair in the back of the room or reading on the rug with a group.) The surface appearance of a casual, relaxed group of children who are busy reading is built on a solid and highly structured foundation.

Perhaps the most important element of that foundation is book selection. Children may need your support to choose enjoyable and appropriate books (for both independent and instructional reading), since choosing a book is not always a simple process for a child. As teacher, you play an important role in modeling and guiding this process.

THE RIGHT LEVEL

While the child's interest and investment are paramount to the acquisition of literacy, the child must also read books that are not too difficult, books which are comfortable, yet challenging. You need to present the child with a range of books at an appropriate level for him or her to achieve success.

Children choose books for a variety of reasons—the cover design is appealing, the illustrations are engaging, a friend is reading the same book, or the story is a familiar one. For some youngsters, free choice is a natural process. The child chooses books that are of interest and that are written at a comfortable reading level. But for most children in the beginning stages of reading, choice needs to be *scaffolded*. In other words, you provide the child with guidance by making recommendations or by providing several book options.

Guiding book selection is a delicate balancing act, as it requires knowing when to provide support, how much guidance to offer, and when to pull back, releasing responsibility to the child. Your ongoing observations of your children's choices and their reading experiences will help you provide guidance.

WHAT SHOULD BE CONSIDERED?

 Providing just the right support involves exploring a variety of factors. When you make a judgment about the appropriateness of the match between the child and the book, consider these issues:

* Is the book to be used for independent reading, for instruction, or for sharing with a friend?

* Is the book too hard, too easy, or just right? Just like the lines from the familiar fairy tale, the child's development as a reader is supported by just the "right" book. Books for independent reading should be interesting, engaging, and comfortable, while books for instruction may be more challenging, requiring more adult support.

* What are the child's interests? What types of stories does the child enjoy? Knowledge of the child's reading history comes into play here, as the teacher considers those stories, authors, and genres enjoyed in the past and how these suggest titles for the future ("Here's another Steig book. I bet Tyesha will love this!").

* What is the purpose for reading? Pleasure? Instruction? Research?

2. Scaffolding the Learning Experience

Your students' language and literacy learning will be supported by your ability to observe your students and to scaffold the learning situation, based on their interests and need to know.

What is scaffolding? It's the ability to structure a learning experience for a child in a way that maximizes the opportunity for success. Parents of young

QUESTIONS FREQUENTLY ASKED ABOUT BOOK SELECTION

How can I help a child choose the right books for reading?

Some children naturally select books that are just right for them, while others need more support. Spend time with children as they make their choices. Listen to a child read aloud a short passage. Discuss the selection process with him or her. Ask, "Is this a good book for you? What makes you say that? How or why did you choose this book?" Later, ask, "How would you rate this book—easy, average, or hard?" These questions help the child become more aware of the selection process. They help the child reflect on the process, encouraging him or her to pick appropriate books.

How do I help a child who consistently chooses books that are too difficult?

You can narrow the range of selections, offering the child a choice from a few appropriate books ("Here are two good books: one on cowboys, the other on life on the prairie. Which do you prefer?"). This gives the child a sense of control and preference and, at the same time, ensures the likelihood of success.

Offering a range of choices is useful in a variety of situations. For example, you might want to introduce a poetry study and provide the students with a sug-gested reading list, asking that they choose from the list for independent reading. Or, you might want to stretch a child's choices by providing a limited range of suggestions of more challenging titles.

Another idea: Provide children with plenty of chances to find out what their classmates are reading. Youngsters may hear about easier books that others have enjoyed.

What if a book is too difficult, but the child really wants to read it?

This often presents a difficult situation. We want to satisfy a child's curiosity and interest, but at the same time, reading at an appropriate level of difficulty is also an important factor in learning to read.

When this occurs, consider trying to find a way to give the child an experience with the chosen book: Pair the child with a friend who might provide support, or find an opportunity for someone to read the book aloud to the child, perhaps at home.

Or, the child could listen to an audiotape while following along in the book. In some cases, reading the book to the child first provides a preview of the story and establishes the context for the child to reread the book on his or her own. Repetition is an excellent way to build fluency and confidence.

How can I find appropriate books for the emerging readers in my class?

Often, emerging readers may memorize a short text after several rereadings, and the text no longer supports further development. Try using the child's own dictated stories as a source of text for reading. This gives the child the background context as well as the interest and investment in the text and can be a wonderful springboard for moving the child beyond the earliest stages of literacy.

Wordless picture books also offer a wonderful opportunity for the child to "read" a book by telling the story aloud, thus promoting oral language fluency and sense of story.

children put this concept into action throughout the day: When they hold the toddler's hand until the child is ready to take those first few steps on his or own; or run alongside a two-wheel bicycle while holding onto the seat until the child is ready to ride off by him- or herself.

Scaffolding is like an apprentice model of learning in which a teacher gives repeated opportunities for demonstration, rehearsal, and trial and error. Scaffolding implies providing just the right combination of these supports. The teacher knows when to pull back as the child becomes more competent, giving the child more responsibility and control.

Closely connected to this concept of providing the right amount of support is the teacher's role as observer. Knowing how and when to scaffold is the result of careful observation and detailed knowedge and understanding of the child. The teaching process is often described as a constant lookout for the "teachable moment."

EXAMPLE OF TEACHABLE MOMENTS

David is an energetic five-year-old who loves coming to school each day. His kindergarten teacher describes him as an enthusiastic learner, easily engaged and filled with questions. David always enjoyed looking at books and listening to stories. By age three, he became interested in the alphabet and writing his own name. At age five, he enjoyed writing his name and the names of his family members, but this was the extent of his interest in writing.

One day, while out on the playground, David passed the time by dropping tiny stones into a tennis ball that had been split open. Mrs. H., his teacher, noticed this activity. When she came over, David asked her, "How many are there?" Mrs. H. suggested that he get a tray to count and guided him to put the stones in piles of tens. This activity continued in the classroom. By the next day David had counted 194 stones. He took a piece of paper and wrote:

100
94

The following day, Mrs. H. sat with him and encouraged him to write a short description, giving the meaning of the numbers. She "stretched" the words, and he wrote:

PBLC N A BL	(pebbles in a ball)
19 10	(19 tens)
nd 4 x 1	(and 4 ones)

David worked with great care and effort, taking some time to complete the writing. His investment in this task was readily apparent. The pebbles experience represented his first attempt at using the written symbol to communicate his message. After this, he began to ask many more questions about how to spell words and to attempt to figure the spelling out for himself.

In this incident, Mrs. H. recognized the opportunity that existed for teaching and learning. Through her response to David's tennis ball on the playground, she showed that she believes in the experiential base for learning and the value of a child's need to know.

She also demonstrated a commitment to helping children learn to read and write through purposeful, meaningful activity. As she slowly said the words, Mrs. H. offered a model of production of speech sounds and corresponding identification of letters to write the word. She offered a model and scaffolded the task of writing the words. As David continues to develop this ability on his own, his need for the teacher model will decrease, and he will identify sound-symbol correspondences with increasing independence. Through careful observation and some trial and error, Mrs. H. will provide support as it is needed.

This example illustrates the relationship between careful observation by the teacher and knowledge of when to provide more explicit, direct instruction. In this case, the direct instruction involved modeling how to say a word slowly, to stretch it so the child can try to spell it. Just a note: There is a considerable amount of phonics instruction embedded in this example, but the phonics is taught within the context of a meaningful task.

HOW IS SCAFFOLDING ACCOMPLISHED?

 There are many ways that scaffolding patterns enter into the daily teaching and learning process. You can provide assistance through

* Modeling and demonstrating

* Providing opportunities for practice and rehearsal

* Prompting and questioning to develop use of strategies for reading

* Arranging flexible groupings and a variety of opportunities for children to work together

* Making available enough options and choices and a range of learning experiences that are engaging, relevant, and meaningful to students

* Focusing on building on a student's strengths

OTHER REAL-LIFE EXAMPLES

Let's look at the ways in which some teachers have helped scaffold experiences in the classroom.

* Anthony is a beginning reader who has a good sight vocabulary and is beginning to use word-analysis knowledge and context clues as strategies for figuring out unknown words. He consistently chooses short, simple books with one to two lines of text per page, and he has read most of these books many times before. His teacher, Mr. B., puts together a folder of five books from a trade book series and asks him to choose from these. By narrowing the choices, Mr. B. has provided the context that will allow Anthony to make a choice that will support his learning to read.

* Danny wants to read *Fox the Brave* by James Marshall. Mrs. L. thinks this may be somewhat difficult, so she decides to read the story to Danny first, thus building on his knowledge of the text and preparing Danny to reread the story with greater fluency and independence.

* Mrs. T. often echo reads with her kindergarten children, both individually and in a large group. She reads a line from the story, thus demonstrating what fluent reading sounds like, and the children reread the line. Through this repetition, the children enjoy the experience of fluent reading and the feeling of success.

* Mrs. H. uses magnetic letters in her kindergarten class to help the children learn to spell their last names. To support their early attempts, she will select the letters to use and ask the child to arrange the letters in order. As the child becomes more competent and familiar with the task, Mrs. H. pulls back her support and lets the child choose the letters from the entire alphabet and arrange them in order.

CHAPTER **5**

Working with Parents

Overview

Literacy and literature extend far beyond the classroom walls and the limits of the school day. This chapter explores ways in which you can work with parents and encourage them as they support their children's progress.

Developing Home-School Communication

Many teachers find that direct involvement is the most effective way to communicate with students' parents. Individual conferences ("Let me show you Lauren's latest story") and larger group formats, such as workshops ("Today let's look at some helpful games you can play at home"), offer opportunities for teachers to share information with moms and dads, and to discuss issues and answer questions regarding how children learn to read and write and how parents might encourage children's literacy at home.

Ongoing, regular contact with parents is key to developing a partnership between home and school. Because the demands of everyday life make it difficult to arrange frequent meetings, parents often appreciate written communication that is clear and to the point. Newsletters or notes offer a vehicle for reporting about children's progress. (Sample newsletters, and other examples of written communication to parents, are included later in this chapter.)

How Can Parents Help?

In my own work with parents, the most frequently asked questions I hear are, "What can I do to improve my child's reading?" and "How can I help my child at home?" General Tips on page 47 address these two questions and suggest ways in which parents can merge their children's home and school literacy experiences. The suggestions are to be used as a resource, as a way for parents to get started. They provide some examples that will stimulate the development of new ideas that emerge naturally from daily classroom life. The ideas are by no means comprehensive; rather, they are selected projects and approaches that have worked for me and families with whom I work. Additional professional resources are provided on pages 57–60.

In this section a general discussion of the role of the parent in supporting the child's growth in literacy will be followed by specific suggestions for reading aloud to youngsters, for observing children's growth, and for involving parents in the assessment process.

THE PARENTS' ROLE: GENERAL TIPS

There are several ways in which parents can provide a literate home environment, one that nurtures an interest in books while at the same time supporting the development of skills for literacy.

1. The best way for parents to help their children grow as readers is to read aloud to them (Anderson, et. al., 1985). A mere fifteen minutes a day— before dinner or at children's bedtime—will greatly increase a child's interest and facility with language and story.

   Parents need to know that they should read aloud to their children not only when they are in the primary grades, but when they are older, too. Hearing a story read aloud—whether a picture book or a chapter book—is pleasurable for children of all ages at all reading levels, from beginning readers to fluent readers.

2. Parents can extend the reading experience by taking their children to the local library regularly. Selecting books from the library helps foster a child's interest in books and develops the habit of reading.

3. Parents are powerful role models for their children. Therefore, children who see the adults around them reading newspapers, books, magazine articles, and letters are more likely to read themselves.

4. Parents should be made aware of natural opportunities for purposeful writing activities in the home, such as writing a note, a shopping list, or a birthday card, or making a sign for the bedroom door. (Children are famous for making signs such as **Genius Within** or **Enter at Your Own Risk.**) Conversation and shared experiences between child and adult offer a rich context for developing literacy.

5. Parents can participate in the assessment process by observing their children's interests and strengths and communicating that information to their child's teacher ("My daughter loves books about sharks"). Their knowledge of their child is important to promoting success in school.

Suggestions for Reading Aloud

In one of the schools in which I work, the teachers and I recently offered an evening workshop for parents of children in the kindergarten through third grades. Our goal was to share a read-aloud experience with the families: to model the shared book-reading experience, to recommend titles, and to enjoy literature together.

In the follow-up discussion with parents, the adults exchanged favorite titles ("I used to love the Grimm's fairy tales as a kid!") and explored what makes a book appealing to a child ("For my son, it's the art"). Mothers and dads reported personal accounts of reading experiences with their children, and a lively discussion occurred.

There was also a question-and-answer period. Questions that spurred discussion included "How do I involve my child in reading?" "What can we talk about with regard to a particular book?" "Should I let my child choose his own books for the reading aloud?" "How can I get my daughter to read a wide range of books?" Parents also expressed interest in receiving book recommendations. (See page 59 for a list of suggested titles shared at one of the read-aloud workshops). In all, parents enjoyed coming to school to share an experience with their children and with other families.

I learned a number of things from the workshop. First, I realized that parents want help in the specifics of selecting and sharing books. Too often in my past conversations with parents and teachers, I found myself taking these details for granted and assuming that discussing the specifics would seem tedious and overbearing. Yet this workshop was a powerful reminder that sharing experiences with books and exchanging recommendations are topics with wide appeal.

Perhaps even more important, this workshop highlighted for me the power of the book to delight, intrigue, and amuse, and reminded me of the allure of sharing a good book with someone else. The social connection provided a powerful context for promoting literacy development. All too often we become wrapped up in issues of learning to read, distancing us from the pleasures and magic of story. In the long run, the focus on enjoying books offers the most powerful motivation to learn to read.

Sample Letter Home

Dear Parents or Caregivers,

This letter provides a summary of the professional literature on the topic of reading aloud.

WHAT THE RESEARCH SAYS:

1. Studies demonstrate that the best way for parents to help their children grow as readers is to read to them.

   "The single most important activity for building knowledge required for eventual success in reading is reading aloud to children."

   (Anderson, R., et. al., *Becoming a Nation of Readers: The Report of the Commission on Reading*, Washington, D.C.: The National Institute of Education, 1985.)

2. Research shows that reading aloud leads to many positive outcomes. For example:

   * *Helps children who are beginning to learn to read*
   * *Improves listening*
   * *Increases a child's ability to read independently (Children are provided with a model of fluent reading and gain a sense of how fluent reading sounds.)*
   * *Increases vocabulary*
   * *Increases reading comprehension*
   * *Improves verbal expression*
   * *Helps children grow as writers*
   * *Increases the quality of independent reading*

   (Michener, D.M., "Test Your Reading Aloud IQ," *The Reading Teacher*, November 1988, 118-122.)

3. Children should have many opportunities to respond to books read aloud, both at home and in school.

   "Engaging students with the story and promoting active involvement with the text are important parts of reading aloud."

   (Anderson, R., et. al., 1985, p. 23.)

We should also keep in mind that books are to be enjoyed, and a response is not always required. We all have times when we just want to sit back, relax, and enjoy the story.

4. Selecting Books to Share

It is important to let your child choose books. Self-selection is a powerful variable in the process of learning to read. Our own excitement about literature will influence our children, and it is important to show our enthusiasm by sharing books we love.

Often, children will choose the same book over and over again, particularly when they are learning to read. The pleasure and sense of accomplishment that accompany these rereadings guide the child into literacy, providing a sense of the joys of reading. Learning to read by memory offers the child a sense of what fluent reading is all about. Children's author Mem Fox characterizes this experience as invaluable and something that parents and teachers should treasure.

I look forward to speaking with you more and sharing your experiences with reading aloud.

Sincerely,

Parents tell us they are grateful for the information we included in these letters home.

Sample Letter Home: How to Make the Most of Reading Aloud

Dear Parents or Caregivers,

You play a crucial role in contributing to your child's growth as a reader. Here are just a few ways that you can make a difference:

1. The single most important thing that parents can do is read to their children. Encourage discussion and active participation.

2. Encourage your child to reread familiar books, stories they have heard or read before. Rereading builds confidence and fluency and allows a child to enjoy those special favorites.

3. When your child chooses to read to you, share in the reading experience, taking turns reading the book or acting out the dialogue together. The main goal is always to have fun and share a book together.

4. Find ways to extend the read-aloud experience by discussing the story, acting out favorite parts, reinventing one's own version of the story, and, perhaps, writing it down and making it into a book or illustrating a favorite part together. Keep a notebook for recording your own stories or a sketchbook for your drawings. Children will enjoy reading through their own collections from time to time, and you will have a wonderful record of your shared experience.

I hope that these ideas stimulate your own thoughts and that you have fun sharing books with your child. I look forward to hearing more about your experiences.

Sincerely,

Sample Letter Home: Sharing the Read-Aloud Experience with Your Child

Dear Parents or Caregivers,

As your child begins to develop as a reader, he or she may want to share the actual reading with you.

1. Wait for your child to initiate reading aloud to you. Many children do not want to read aloud to their parents until they feel quite confident and competent. This is OK; it doesn't mean that growth hasn't occurred. Although it is often difficult, the best thing we can do as parents is remain patient and continue to share books together, to read to our children in a relaxed, comfortable, and enjoyable setting. In the early stages of reading development, we can help relieve some of the pressure by reminding ourselves that it important for the child to <u>want</u> to read to us, and that it is alright if this does not occur.

2. Some suggestions, once your child does begin to read to you:

   * *Many children enjoy taking turns, alternating the actual reading. This can feel much more comfortable to them than having the entire spotlight.*

   * *Accept substitutions for words in the actual text whenever they keep the meaning. This is often a sign of fluent reading and shows that the reader is searching for and constructing meaning, and clearly this should be reinforced. Only when the child substitutes a word for another and the meaning is changed or unclear, should you supply the correct word.*

   * *If a child has difficulty with a word, before telling her what the word is, encourage the child to think about what might make sense or what might come next, or to look at the illustrations for a clue.*

Reading with your child should always be an enjoyable time for both of you. The focus should always be on making meaning and enjoying the shared reading experience. Keep in mind that even as your child becomes a more independent and fluent reader, the pleasures and benefits of reading aloud to him or her continue.

Sincerely,

Recommending Books for Reading Aloud

In my experience, the most effective way to learn about good books is to talk with other people—parents, teachers, family members, neighbors, children, and friends. It is through these personal recommendations that we learn why a book is appealing and what makes the reading experience pleasurable. A personal review is a powerful source of finding out more about great books for reading aloud.

I mentioned earlier that parents are often interested in seeing recommended reading lists. We, as teachers, are in good positions to provide parents with these. For this reason, I have included on page 59 one such list. Keep in mind: For every great book that is included, another is likely to be excluded. Book lists are useful resources and should be used as such. When I put a list of recommended readings together, I always view it as a work in progress. Great new books are always being published and should be considered as well.

Suggestions for Involving Parents in School Activities

In addition to sharing ideas for ways parents can support the development of literacy at home, there are many wonderful ways to invite them to actively share in their child's experience in school. Here are just a few ideas:

* Invite parents to a "read-in." This can be a class event or one that represents the collective effort of several different classes or grade levels. Invite parents, teachers, and children to an afternoon or evening of sharing literature and experiences with books.

* Invite parents to a celebration of poetry. Children enjoy learning about poetry, engaging in choral and dramatic readings, and writing their own poems. In Denise Gilbert's third-grade class, after a yearlong study of poetry and photography, the children take a series of photographs and select one as a springboard for poetry writing. Each child carefully crafts a poem to accompany the photograph. The classroom is transformed into an art gallery, and the parents are invited to the opening—an "art event"!

* Invite parents to the classroom to read aloud a favorite book from their childhood. Children too can share their memories of favorite books. This can be extended with the book *Once Upon a Time: Celebrating the Magic of Children's Books in Honor of the Twentieth Anniversary*

of Reading is Fundamental (New York: G. P. Putnam's Sons, 1986). This is a collection of memoirs by well-known authors and illustrators about early experiences with literature. Writers Jack Prelutsky, Natalie Babbitt, Judy Blume, Dr. Seuss, Maurice Sendak, Shel Silverstein, and Tomie dePaola are just a few of those included. In Dolores Thompson's third-grade class, in fact, children were eager to share their recollections of favorite books and enjoyed listening to excerpts from them. Their enthusiasm resulted in their expressing some of their memories through writing and drawing. One student was so inspired by Jack Prelutsky's poem in the anniversary collection mentioned above that he wrote his own version, hoping to inspire some of the first- and second-graders to capture their memories on paper.

✳ Share "literacy" stories across the curriculum through weekly or monthly newsletters. Maureen Montone sends home a weekly newsletter, capturing the highlights and giving parents the inside view of life in the classroom (see page 60). The newsletter is appreciated by all, and even the children take pleasure in reading it.

✳ Invite parents to a holiday celebration. Let the children be the party planners—making all the arrangements, "from soup to nuts." The children can make invitations, create a list of "things to do," choose recipes for the refreshments, and, perhaps, plan to share some of their own writing or artwork (related to the holiday theme) at the event.

In Barbara Tessler's kindergarten class, the children invited their mothers to a special Mother's Day brunch. Youngsters created personalized invitations, planned the menu, and decorated the classroom for the big event. The mothers did not want the brunch to end (always a sign of successful entertaining). As the festivities were winding down, some of the children began to show their moms around the room, pointing out their work, special class projects, and favorite activities. One child enthusiastically pulled his mother over to the bookshelves, eager to show her his favorite books, and soon they were cuddled on the couch reading *Dinosaur Garden* by Liza Donnelly. Within minutes, the idea caught on, and all around the room, mothers and children found a cozy spot to share a good book. It was a perfect way to end the morning.

✳ Encourage parents to look for natural opportunities to share written communication with their children. Children often enjoy receiving a note in their lunch box or a surprise note at the breakfast table. Back-to-school night always offers an excellent opportunity for children to write a note for their parents and for parents to respond so that the child receives the letter in school the next morning.

Rob is learning, much to his delight, that he can communicate with his parents through letter-writing.

* Feature an author-of-the month and invite parents to join a group discussion. Select popular read-aloud authors, such as Eric Carle, Tomie dePaola, Cynthia Rylant, Shel Silverstein, or William Steig. Ask each group to read aloud one of the books from the collection and to share their personal responses with each other. Small groups of three to four parents and three to four students generally work best. Assign a leader for each group (a parent or child, depending on the grade level) and provide the leader with a list of questions to keep the discussion going. Ask the groups to generate suggestions for authors to feature in the future, and keep the book groups going.

* Invite a children's author to the classroom and host an Author Talk, including parents in the festivities. Before the author's visit, ask parents and children to share books by that author and, if possible, make books available for them to borrow and read aloud at home.

Involving Parents in Self-Reflection and the Assessment Process

Parents play an important role in the assessment process. Their observations and intimate knowledge of their child are important aspects of the home-school partnership. Together, parents and teachers can share observations and develop ways to best support a child's growth. Encourage parents to share information about

* General interests

* Ways the child enjoys spending time at home

* How the child approaches homework

* How the child feels about school and what information the child shares about school

* Friends, play dates

* Relations with siblings

Workshops and questionnaires can be helpful tools in helping parents to reflect on their own experiences learning to read and write, on how they engage in literate activity as adults, on their goals for their children, and on ways they engage in literate activity with their children. Sample surveys and questionnaires and a newsletter are included on the following pages.

The questionnaire on page 57 was used as part of The Read-Aloud Project, The Mamaroneck Public School, Spring 1995, a project funded by The Teacher Institute of the Mamaroneck Public Schools. Project members include Ellen Brooks, Patricia Fanning, Barry Koski, and Jeannine Miller, Mamaroneck Avenue School.

FALL PARENT OR CAREGIVER/CHILD SURVEY

1. At home, my child enjoys

   _____.

2. At home, my child spends most of his/her time

   _____.

3. The last time I read to my child was

   _____.

4. I read to my child approximately
   _____ every day.   _____ several times a month.
   _____ more than once a week.   _____ less than once a month.

5. My child enjoys listening to books about

   _____.

6. Some of my child's favorite books are

   _____.

7. My child's response to being read to is

   _____.

8. When we read together, the books are selected by

   _____.

9. I think it is important to read to your child because

   _____.

10. The most important thing I do with my child is

   _____.

Parents are often grateful for an opportunity to familiarize the teacher with the child's interests.

Exploring Your Own Literacy

1. Describe your early experiences with books. (If possible, think back to the pre-school years.)

   _____

   _____

   _____

   _____

2. Did you have any favorite books as a child? List favorites that you remember. Include anything else that comes to mind about the book or why you remember it.

   _____

   _____

   _____

3. Describe your current experience as a reader and writer. When do you engage in these activities? For what purposes?

   _____

   _____

   _____

4. What five books would you consider "most significant" to your life? (These can be from your childhood or adulthood years.) List them and tell why each is important to you.

   _____

   _____

   _____

It's often fun for parents to write about their own book experiences.

June 199__

Dear Parents or Caregivers,

Attached is a list of recommended books for reading aloud. These titles were shared at the May "read-aloud" workshop.

Thanks again for your participation, and have fun reading!

Sincerely,
Barry Koski, Ellen Brooks, Pat Fanning, and Jeannine Miller
The Mamaroneck Avenue School
Mamaroneck, New York

Teachers' Recommended Book List

Hans Christian Andersen, *The Emperor's New Clothes, Little Red Riding Hood*, etc.

Natalie Babbitt, *Truck Everlasting, Knee Knock Rise*

Lynne Reid Banks, *The Indian in the Cupboard, The Secret of the Indian, The Return of the Indian, The Mystery of the Cupboard*

John Bellairs, *The House with a Clock in Its Wall*

Judy Blume, *Superfudge, Freckle Juice, Tales of a Fourth Grade Nothing, The One in the Middle Is a Green Kangaroo*

Marc Brown, *Arthur's Teacher Trouble, Arthur Goes to Camp, Arthur Babysits, Arthur's Nose*, others

Roald Dahl, *Charlie and the Chocolate Factory, James and the Giant Peach, Fantastic Mr. Fox, George's*

Marvelous Medicine Show, Matilda, The Witches, The BFG, others

Madeline L'Engle, *Many Waters, The Wind in the Door, A Swiftly Tilting Planet, A Wrinkle in Time*

Ruth Stiles Gannett, *My Father's Dragon, Elmer and the Dragon, The Dragons of Blueland*

Phyllis Naylor, *Shiloh*

Gary Paulsen, *Hatchet, Dancing Carl, Dogsong*

Jon Scieszka, *The True Story of the Three Little Pigs*

Jerry Spinelli, *Maniac Magee*

Chris Van Allsburg, *The Polar Express, Jumanji, The Garden of Abdul Gasazi*

E. B. White, *Charlotte's Web, Stuart Little, Trumpet of the Swans*

Elizabeth Winthrop, *The Castle in the Attic*, others

Parents and children often raced to the library over the weekend to pick up the books we recommended.

Week of June _____

Dear Parents or Caregivers,

We've been reading a short book together called *Mostly Magic* by Ruth Chew. This book is a personal favorite of mine, and the children seem to love it as well. Ruth Chew has written many short chapter books that are quick and easy to read and are also great fun, as they involve magic and mystery. They seem to capture the imagination of children young and old. I still read and enjoy these books, so many of the children might also.

I am currently working on a book list that I will hand out before Friday to give you some leads for summer reading, but keep in mind that the best leads will probably come from your child. Since one of my goals for reading is to have each child know himself/herself as a reader so he/she can make good choices for reading, I'd love to see a dialogue about reading continue over the summer. Talking with your child (about books they have liked, favorite authors, topics of interest) and visiting the library or bookstores together are wonderful ways to foster their growth as readers. You might even want to pick a book that you and your child can read together (not necessarily simultaneously, though this is always great fun and a viable option, too!) and discuss. You might try including an older brother or sister, an aunt or uncle, a grandma or grandpa and forming a family book group of your own! Your child can tell you how to do it and would probably enjoy doing so!

As part of our study of fiction, we have continued working on telling our own versions of William Steig's *Sylvester and the Magic Pebble*. Children look closely at the elements of the story—the significant events, the conflict, the climax, the resolution—in order to create their own adaptation to tell. In a sense, they are "reliving" a well-crafted and masterful fiction piece, and this helps give them a firsthand knowledge of the elements of a good story.

Time to sign off again. Until next week...

Sincerely,
Maureen Montone

A newsletter can be handwritten or set on a computer or with a typewriter. No matter what, it's a great way to reach families at home.

CHAPTER 6

Literacy Stories

et's look at the ways in which practicing teachers find ways to support children's development of specific skills and strategies. The following five case studies illustrate how ongoing observation, documentation, and reflection lead to a child's understanding of a book or a teacher's understanding of a child, which, in turn, allows the teacher to build on the child's strengths.

Susan

BACKGROUND/ASSESSMENT INFORMATION

Susan is in the second grade. Early in the year, Susan's classroom teacher, Mrs. R., had several questions about Susan's reading. Mrs. R. invited the reading teacher, Mrs. B., into the classroom to read with the girl. What could the teachers do to promote Susan's success?

Mrs. R.'s reading program is literature-based, with an emphasis on the connections between reading, writing, listening, and speaking. The classroom library is filled with a range of books, and children are encouraged to select their own books for reading. During the daily reading period, children can read on their own or with partners. During that time Mrs. R. conferences with individual children or with small groups. Specific skills and strategies for reading are taught within the context of oral reading. In follow-up mini-lessons, specific skills—from phonics to comprehension—are taught. Literature discussion groups meet at least once a week, and children write weekly in their response journals.

What did Mrs. R find when reading with Susan? Results of oral reading samples (see Running Record, page 63) and descriptive observations revealed that Susan used few strategies for reading. She often relied on "looking" at the whole word, rather than using such devices as noting prefixes or suffixes. The girl also relied on adult support, rather than her own resources, to decipher unknown words.

Name: Susan

Teacher: Mrs. R.

Date: 9/16

Billy Goats Gruff (Ladybird series)

(H) Here are
the / billy (H) goats Gruff.

rereading - has read this story several times before and is highly familiar with the plot.

/ (H) This is
little billy goat Gruff.
He likes to jump. /

This is
/ (H) middle-sized
billy goat Gruff.
He likes to / eat (H) grass. (H)

- waits for help

- gave meaning prompt, but did not take a guess

(H) Here is a bridge.
A / big (H) troll
lives
under the bridge.

- prompted to use beginning "b" sound, but this did not help.

The billy goats Gruff
(H) want to go
over the bridge
for some grass.

Key

(H) - teacher supplied help

/ - indicates hesitation by child.

While administering a running record for Susan, we realized that the child needed to develop more strategies for figuring out words.

THE INSTRUCTIONAL PLAN

Mrs. R. decided to spend some additional time reading with Susan on a one-to-one basis, devoting about two to three sessions per week. During that time she would present to Susan short, simple books; model various reading strategies; and introduce word-analysis techniques. The word-study work combined phonic elements ("Those letters blend together to form this sound"), linguistic elements, and awareness of structural analysis ("Do you see that both words end with -ing?").

The teacher encouraged Susan to write her reaction to the books, to use magnetic letters to make words, and to play word-making and sentence-making games. The words for these games were taken directly from the books and connected back to the reading of the stories.

Mrs. R. kept detailed notes describing these reading sessions, recording Susan's general progress, interests, and strategies for reading.

MID-YEAR REVIEW OF PROGRESS: DEVELOPING A LITERACY PROFILE

In February, Mrs. R. reviewed the value of one-to-one support, as growth was not evident. Given the enormous effort on the part of the teacher, this lack of growth was puzzling and troublesome. The teacher expressed concern because, although Susan loved listening to stories, she seemed reluctant to read independently.

Mrs. R. and Mrs. B. carefully examined Susan's work, collected over time. Together they brainstormed new possibilities. Based on Denny Taylor's work on literacy profiles, the teachers posed key questions that framed their study of Susan's work samples. The questions were

* What kinds of literacy activity does Susan choose to do on her own?

* How does she construct and use language?

* What does Susan like to do? What can she do, and when is she successful?

Susan enjoyed listening to stories, drawing pictures, telling stories, and, to some degree, writing. But she did not seem willing to invest herself in actually learning to read. Her teachers agreed they were pushing the issue by presenting the very activity that the youngster was trying to avoid.

Susan's reaction was often extreme; at reading time, she would hide behind her books, sinking slowly into her seat, once even retreating to a safe space underneath her desk. Most of the students looked forward to reading time, hoping to be noticed and to be invited to read alone with the teacher.

SHIFTING THE FOCUS TO WRITING

 Mrs. R. and Mrs. B. decided that they were headed in the wrong direction. They discussed highlighting writing and using this as a way in to reading. Mrs. R. noted that Susan enjoyed drawing and writing her own stories, although the actual writing was difficult for her.

Mrs. R. began to work with Susan in rewriting her own stories. Later, the stories were typed and used as a source for Susan's reading. Follow-up games and activities to build word-analysis knowledge were soon added; specific words and phonic/linguistic elements were selected from the actual stories.

With time, the teachers noticed a striking change in Susan's involvement. She was much more engaged and focused when the source of reading was her own writing. This shift occurred at the end of February.

THE ROLE OF THE ARTS

In early March, another significant event occurred. Susan participated in the class play, "Sleeping Beauty." She read the story many times and volunteered to take the part of the narrator. She was involved and excited about the project. She worked with Mrs. R., reading her part. There was much activity and excitement as the class joined together making props, creating costumes, and rehearsing. The class hosted several successful performances for other classes.

MONITORING PROGRESS: AN UPDATE

By April, Susan was reading with ease and confidence. She especially enjoyed books from HarperCollins's *I Can Read* series. She was willing to attempt words on her own, used a variety of strategies for reading, and discussed the stories with great interest, often making connections to her own life. At reading time, she sat up and smiled at the teacher, and the invitation to read together was accepted with openness and pleasure.

Susan moved from avoiding reading and writing to interest in communicating through writing and to a genuine interest in books. Perhaps even more striking was the openness she started exhibiting, showing a confidence to takes risks and to take on the responsibility for her own learning.

Susan's progress and pride in her own reading were a reminder that confidence is a powerful aspect of learning. The pattern of her progress also demonstrated that growth is not always linear, nor does it occur in uniform increments. Susan was, no doubt, making progress all along, but she did not make herself visible for many months.

PLANNING FOR THE FUTURE

 Recognizing Susan's growing competence and confidence, her teachers developed plans for extending her learning in the coming weeks:

1. Susan's success with the reading series indicated that these books were useful resources for promoting growth. The teachers agreed that the amount of time Susan spends reading is very important. The more she reads, the more she will grow as a reader. Susan would be introduced to many books, such as *Come Back Amelia Bedelia, Frog and Toad Are Friends, Frog and Toad Together, Harry and the Lady Next Door, Play Ball, Amelia Bedelia*, and *Ten Copycats in a Boat.* In addition, the *Henry and Mudge* series (Aladdin) and the *Fox* series (Puffin Easy-to-Read) were also recommended as books that might provide more of a challenge. In all cases, Susan would be given three to four selections to choose from.

2. Susan's interest in fairy tales should be explored as this may offer another genre for her reading. She might enjoy reading different versions of one story, tales told from another point of view, or multicultural versions of familiar fairy tales. Opportunities for responding through drawing or creating dramatic re-enactments of the fairy tales with others in the class should be encouraged. Extending Susan's experience with fairy tales may provide a way to extend her experience with more difficult books, knowing that she will draw on her own prior knowledge of the story.

3. Reading aloud to Susan continues to be very important. While Susan demonstrates considerable progress in becoming an independent and fluent reader, the benefits of reading aloud to her are as important as ever.

4. Susan enjoys listening to poetry. Her favorite children's poets are Jack Prelutsky and Shel Silverstein. Given Susan's interest in dramatic activity, poetry may offer a springboard for choral reading and other

dramatic activity. Mrs. R. suggested extending the class experience with drama to poetry. The children were immersed in reading poetry, and Mrs. B. gave them frequent opportunities to practice crafting their own poems. She suggested that the children organize and produce a poetry-reading event as their culminating activity.

WHAT WORKED

The key to Susan's growth was the focus on strengths, a result of the ongoing, descriptive observation in the classroom. Through their professional collaboration, Mrs. R. and Mrs. B. came to recognize that drawing, telling stories, and dramatizations are powerful activities that offer hooks into literacy.

Tommy

OBSERVING THE CHILD

Mrs. T announces quiet reading time, and Tommy shuffles his feet, moving slowly toward the bookshelves. He returns to his desk with an action-hero comic book, the latest rage among the elementary school boys. The language of the text is sophisticated and challenging.

Mrs. T. walks over to Tommy's desk, inviting him to read with her. Noting that Tommy has selected a text of interest, but one that is well beyond both his independent and instructional levels, she suggests, "Why don't I read some of this to you, and we can also find another story to read together." Tommy listens intently as Mrs. T. reads several pages from the comic book. He carefully studies the illustrations and freely comments on the action of the story. His involvement is obvious.

SCAFFOLDING CHOICES

When it is time to read another selection, Mrs. T. gives Tommy a choice of four books from a supplementary reading series. Mrs. T. is providing Tommy with an opportunity to choose, but at the same time she is providing several choices that will be comfortable yet challenging for him to read aloud. In this way, she is scaffolding the self-selection process by guiding Tommy into appropriate choices for reading.

Cooperatively, but without enthusiasm, Tommy chooses *Morris the Moose* and he begins to read with relative ease. Some support from Mrs. T. is needed, but the text is comfortable for Tommy. He reads with an overall sense of confidence and with fluency.

When they finish the story, Mrs. T. suggests they do some follow-up writing. "Oh," Tommy remarks. "That was boring, but I like to write the sentences." He was referring to a follow-up activity that has become a familiar routine. Mrs. T. dictates sentences from the story and uses this as an opportunity to further develop word-analysis knowledge. Together they work on several sentences and individual words, examining linguistic patterns, aspects of phonic analysis, and sentence structure. Then Tommy rereads a short passage from the story. At the conclusion of their time together, Tommy returns to the action-hero comic, inviting a friend to read with him.

ASSESSING PROGRESS: THE ROLE OF ACTIVE INVOLVEMENT

Later that afternoon Mrs. T. reviews Tommy's progress. She notes that he enjoys writing with the same consistency with which he rejects reading.

Mrs. T. thinks about Tommy's interests. Immediately she considers his interest in animals and in drawing; he often draws for long periods of time, carefully attending to the detail of his work. On the other hand, Tommy seems to distance himself from the reading experience.

A FOCUS ON STRENGTHS

Aiming to promote a greater interest in reading, Mrs. T. decides to introduce nonfiction to Tommy, perhaps linking this to a writing experience.

She floods the classroom with animal books and, when possible, links this genre with the science/social studies curriculum. Tommy's favorites include books about monkeys and apes, about jungle animals, and about the rain forest.

The interest in these books spreads fast throughout the classroom. Several of the children decide to make their own book, and Tommy watches with interest. Mrs. T. observes his interest and casually suggests that he might want to create his own book too. Tommy agrees; his enthusiasm actually takes Mrs. T. by surprise. He begins to work on the first draft at a table with several other children. While they each work on their own project, the children freely exchange comments and offer to help each other. Tommy works for days, alternating between writing and illustrating the text. This was the first time he has written so much on his own, and his investment is readily apparent.

WHAT WORKED

Mrs. T. is delighted with Tommy's involvement and senses that this experience is key to opening the door to his growing interest in books. This project allowed Mrs. T. to recognize that Tommy's path would not be a traditional one. For him, the key was literacy through writing and drawing, and pulling back on the reading was an important step. When he did read, nonfiction offered the most useful link to books and reading.

Michael

BACKGROUND: A FIRST-GRADE CLASSROOM

Mrs. W's first-grade class offers many rich opportunities for children to engage in literate activity. She provides each of the twenty-two children with a wide range of choices, and she is continually looking for ways to increase the available literature in the classroom. In addition to independent and partner reading, Mrs. W. tries to read individually with each child in the class.

Early in the year, Michael did not want to read individually with Mrs. W. He showed this in many ways, verbally and nonverbally, yet he was very interested in books, and he would "hang around" listening to other children read with the teacher. Over the last few weeks, Mrs. W. has devoted more time for one-to-one reading with Michael. She feels that, although reading seems to be a struggle for him, he is on the brink of a breakthrough. The individual attention will provide the extra support he needs.

In addition to a wide variety of rich literacy experiences, Michael reads with Mrs. W. two to three times each week. She provides him with several book choices, including books that will encourage success and provide her with opportunities to model and provide basic strategies for reading. Michael is always willing and cooperative, yet at the same time, he is reserved in this one-to-one reading situation. From time to time, the teacher senses that the boy is nervous. He often stumbles or stutters over words that he knows, and his facial expression reveals tension.

PROVIDING INDIVIDUAL ATTENTION

Mrs. W. wonders if Michael is comparing himself to some of his friends in the class who seem to be moving into literacy with great ease. He is highly social and well-liked; the children in the class often seek him out during free play and small-group activity. Perhaps, she thinks, the individual attention will result in his growth as a reader, and the signs of discomfort will fade.

RE-EVALUATING THE INSTRUCTIONAL PLAN

Mrs. W. pursues the one-to-one sessions, but Michael continues to show signs of nervousness. Mrs. W. reviews her records of their work together and decides to try a different tactic: emphasizing writing over reading.

The next day, Mrs. W. announces quiet reading time and slowly makes her way over to Michael. He is sitting at the round table in the corner of the classroom, looking at a book with his friend Scott. She approaches quietly, observing that the two boys are looking at the book, laughing and chatting freely with each other. Michael and Scott are reading *Pickle Things*, a zany rhyme by Marc Brown about pickle ears and pickle toes, pickle balls and pickle bats, and just about any pickle thing you might imagine. Mrs. W. sits down at the table, asking if she might share in the fun. The boys readily agree, and they begin taking turns reading. The process is quite natural, and it is clear that the humor is the big attraction. Reading serves a purpose of allowing them to enjoy the silliness; the boys are immersed in the book and filled with laughter, and "reading" is clearly in the background. The text is brief; the rhyme and the strong picture clues allow the beginning reader to be highly successful. Both boys read with fluency and ease; several times each helps the other to figure out a word.

READING PARTNERS

After reading, Mrs. W. shares several books that she had selected earlier to use with Michael. She decides to read again with both boys; they were working so well together that she hated to break up the collaboration. Michael chooses *Mrs. Brice's Mice*, a book that he had started the day before with Mrs. W. Michael turns to Scott and says, "You'll like this one too. It's really funny."

Michael reads fluently and with independence. He shows evidence of a variety of strategies, and several times, he monitors his own reading and makes the appropriate self-corrections. As he reads, he smiles, expressing his pleasure and finding great humor in the story, and several times he initiates conversation about the events in the story. When they finish the book, Michael and Scott ask if they could continue to read together, and Mrs. W. replies, "Of course."

The next day, Scott and Michael choose Rita Gelman's *More Spaghetti, I Say* to read together, another story full of humor and zaniness. Mrs. W. reads with them for a few minutes and finds that Michael continues to read with considerable fluency and great pleasure. Upon further reflection, it becomes apparent to her that Michael is not responding to the one-to-one sessions. Rather, his strengths are more apparent when he is relaxed and sharing reading with a friend. The result: Mrs. W. began to read with both boys regularly, providing the same instructional program in the small group as she had in the individual sessions, and Michael continued with great success.

WHAT WORKED

Michael's story reveals the importance of the social context for reading and the role of individual interest and investment. In this instance, the interest was in humor, a genre enjoyed by many children. Generally, we expect children to benefit from one-to-one attention, and while Michael's case may be more of an exception than the rule, it is an excellent reminder of the need to closely observe children and understand their interests, their strengths, and the conditions that best support their learning.

Evan

BACKGROUND

When Evan was in first grade, he was deeply attached to the *Henry and Mudge* books by Cynthia Rylant. His Irish setter, Max, reminded him of Mudge, although Max was not quite as big and imposing as Mudge. Evan's affection for this fictional character was even greater because his Aunt Betty sent him his first Henry and Mudge book as a gift.

In school, Evan regularly chose *Henry and Mudge* during quiet reading time, content to muse over the pictures and construct the story in his mind. Mrs. F. reinforced his interest, but she was concerned because the text was too difficult and did not provide Evan with the opportunity to further develop his strategies for reading. She attempted to suggest alternatives, guiding Evan into selections that provided a more appropriate instructional level. But Evan was not interested. He firmly restated his love of Henry and Mudge and his determination to stick with these stories.

USING DICTATED STORIES FOR READING INSTRUCTION

Mrs. F. decided to use the *Henry and Mudge* series as a springboard for Evan writing his own Henry and Mudge story. Evan was receptive to this invitation; he dictated his story, and Mrs. F. acted as scribe. Later, she typed the story; the next day Evan illustrated it. When it was complete, Mrs. F. used Evan's story as a text for reading instruction and encouraged him to reread his story with a friend during quiet reading time. Evan responded with enthusiasm.

MONITORING PROGRESS

Evan's progress was slow, but steady. By the end of first grade, Evan enjoyed reading and writing and was highly invested in the process of learning to read, although he was reading below grade level. But he was more willing to read new titles suggested by Mrs. F. As a result, he read a wide range of books at an appropriate instructional level. Evan showed his desire to read in many ways. By the end of second grade, he was reading on grade level, demonstrating his interest in both fiction and nonfiction.

UNDERSTANDING EVAN'S GROWTH

Although Evan's growth spurt seemed to occur in second grade, in fact, he was making great strides all through first grade, following a less traditional route to learning to read. There are many facets to his success.

Mrs. F.'s first-grade classroom was filled with books. Over the years, the teacher had developed a library rich in resources. Yet the wide range of possibilities was not key in Evan's case. Evan's story reminds us of the powerful role of the learner in taking responsibility for one's own learning and the teacher's role in closely observing each student, adapting knowledge, resources, and professional experience to the needs of each individual child. Mrs. F. acknowledged Evan's interest and overall confidence in himself and adapted the instructional program in a way that promoted investment and success.

WHAT WORKED

Underlying Evan's story of success is a reflective practitioner who carefully observed the child, building on his interests and strengths. When faced with the conflict between the child's choice and the difficulty of the book, Mrs. F. revised the teaching situation, finding a new hook, a new way in to building skills, strategies, and reading fluency. As Evan learned through his own stories, Mrs. F. gradually began to introduce new books, texts less challenging than *Henry and Mudge*. Evan was more receptive because he felt more confident and able to exert a reasonable degree of control over the reading material.

Annie

LEARNING TO READ NATURALLY

This chapter would not be complete without a closer look at those children who seem to learn to read naturally, without direct instruction, often learning long before they enter school. We tend to take their learning for granted, without realizing how much we can learn about the making of a successful reader. Annie's story is a wonderful example of a child who learned to read with ease, engaging with books and surrounded by a highly literate environment.

BACKGROUND

I remember walking into Mrs. M.'s second-grade class at quiet reading time; some days were quieter than others, but the one constant was Annie reading at her desk. Relaxed and at ease with her book, Annie seemed unaware of the activity around her and immersed in her book. Always responsive to inquiries about her reading, Annie would chat freely and then return to her book, displaying a strong sense of self-direction, motivation, and interest.

To understand Annie's literacy development, I decided to interview her mother (Lisa), looking for details about her earliest experiences with books and, perhaps, some moments that might offer insight into her growth as a reader.

The Early Years: Family Literacy

Lisa remembers reading to Annie when the girl was eight months old, cuddling up on the couch before bedtime. Annie loved classics like *Pat the Bunny* and *Goodnight Moon* and was content to listen and study the pictures for long periods of time. She became used to her mother's style of reading *Goodnight Moon*, anticipating the words in the text and Lisa's intonation and inflection. If Lisa deviated, Annie immediately ordered, "Read it the same way, Mommy." At a very young age, Annie learned the pleasures of shared reading, the joy of story, and the expressive form of a story read aloud. She had a natural sense of the way a story should sound and had developed an inner feeling for the flow of fluent reading. Annie's love of books continued, and her interest was nurtured by the daily routine of reading aloud and frequent walks to the library to check books out and attend story hour.

Lisa recalled some of Annie's early favorites, reminiscing how many of these early stories and characters became woven into her everyday life. For Annie, literature opened the door to new worlds to explore and offered a way to mediate her own experience in the world. *The Carrot Seed* sparked her desire to plant her own, in spite of Lisa's coaxing to plant a heartier seed with a better chance of survival. Annie loved to dress up and frequently asked for *Go, Dog, Go,* waiting for her favorite part when the dogs dress up in their fancy hats. Annie would repeat the familiar line, "Do you like my hat?" Later, *Angelina Ballerina* became a favorite as Annie identified with the struggles of Angelina and developed a special fondness for the character.

Lisa and her husband, Richard, continued reading to Annie. Her interest in books continued to grow when she went off to kindergarten. Lisa commented that she wasn't really sure when Annie could read on her own because they read to her so often, for the purpose of enjoyment rather than the goal of teaching Annie to read. Pleasure and personal connections marked their reading time together.

The Primary Years: Moving Into Literacy

In her kindergarten classroom, Annie frequently took a book and settled in a corner of the room. At first, Mrs. D., her teacher, thought Annie was enjoying the illustrations, but as she observed carefully, she noticed Annie's eyes moving back and forth across the page, as if taking in the print. One day Mrs. D. asked Annie about the story, and their discussion made it clear that Annie was reading text and pictures on her own. As they

Annie expresses her interests through her writing.

MY MOM LIKES to WRAK LUS

There once was a Brontosaurus. His name was Alex.

read together, Mrs. D. learned that Annie could read many simple books with fluency and ease. At the mid-year parent-teacher conference, Mrs. D. noted that self-selection was very important: Annie liked to choose her own books and then showed great interest in sharing her reading aloud. In contrast, if Mrs. D. chose the book, Annie responded in a gentle, but firm, manner, "No, thanks. I don't want to read that."

In kindergarten, Annie also enjoyed writing and dictating stories. She often wrote about her family or about dinosaurs, a topic that she enjoyed reading about.

First grade was characterized by a somewhat traditional reading program, with great emphasis on phonics worksheets and multiple-choice exercises for comprehension instruction. While the program was also literature-based, the books were chosen by the teacher, without room for self-selection or input by the children. Annie reluctantly read the assigned books, continuing at home to read the books she truly treasured. She enjoyed *Charlotte's Web*, *The Little House on the Prairie* series, and others much more challenging than those assigned in school.

In second grade, the classroom program was more child-centered, offering a rich context to support Annie's growth as a reader and writer. Mrs. M. scheduled a daily quiet reading time, encouraging students to choose their own books and to share suggestions with each other. From time to time, Mrs. M. recommended books to Annie, hoping to expand her awareness of literature. The reading time was flexible: Students could read on their own or with a partner, and Mrs. M. conferenced with small groups or individual children. Annie was always buried in her book, generally choosing to read on her own. Favorites included *The Wayside School* series, other books from the *The Lit-*

tle House on the Prairie series, and *All-of-a-Kind Family.* (See excerpt from Annie's book log for more titles.) Mrs. M. understood Annie's strengths and recognized her need for options and opportunities to self-select her own reading material.

WHAT WORKED

Annie learned to read quite naturally and seemed to do it all on her own. And yet the context was key to providing the opportunity for growth. In many ways, Annie's is a familiar story. Her experience further validates much of what we already know about the power of the literate home environment and specific aspects of that context that promote the development of literacy: the importance of reading aloud, providing a social context for literacy, encouraging self-selection, and recognizing the role of repetition in learning.

Name Annie Witten	Grade 2M

Homework Reading Assignments
Recommended times – 1/2 hr. daily

	Title
Mon.	Little house In the big Woods, Launa Wilder.
Tues. Poetry	Ride a purple Pelican. Jack Prelutsky.
Wed.	Pippi goes on bored Astrin Lindren
Thurs.	Pippi in the South Seas Astrin Lindren

On the weekend, please use the Public Library
to select books and to browse.
Thank you.
G.M.M.

Parent's Signature

In her log, Annie keeps track of books read.

When asked to reflect on what worked, Lisa responded, "Osmosis," but after a few minutes reflecting, it became clear that immersion was at the heart of Annie's experience. She was immersed in books, story, and language...and in sharing these activities with her family in a relaxed and warm environment. Annie's interest, investment, and strong desire to learn and take responsibility for her own learning shaped her experience and marked her growth.

KEEP IN MIND

In these sample cases a variety of approaches were used to encourage the development of motivated and independent readers. Successful experiences grew out of a focus on self-selection and regular opportunities to read; through writing, drawing, and the arts; through the social context; and by using the child's own dictated stories as a source of text for reading. Through ongoing observation and a focus on each child's strengths and interests, each of these teachers found a way into literacy for their student.

FOR FURTHER READING
Taylor, Denny, "Teaching Without Testing," *English Education, 22,*
    February 1990, 3-74.

CHAPTER 7

Suggested Children's Books

Finding the Right Books

When Mr. H., a first-grade teacher, decided to move toward literature-based reading instruction, he examined his classroom library. The collection seemed sizable and well stocked, he felt. He had a range of books at varying levels and felt confident about meeting the needs of his students.

Mr. H. began the year with great enthusiasm, sharing books and encouraging students to make their own choices. The children seemed responsive as they eagerly explored the bookshelves, curious and chattering. But gradually, as Mr. H. got to observe his students in many situations, he began to re-evaluate the book collection. He noticed how few titles were really appropriate for those children at the earliest stages of learning to read. With the help of his colleagues, Mr. H. gathered together a stack of books with simple text and predictable patterns. The presence of "easy" books was immediately obvious and dramatic. Mr. H. was a firm believer that the best way to teach children to read was to engage them in purposeful, meaningful, pleasurable, and successful reading experiences. Without books at the appropriate level, this could not occur.

Mr. H. recognized the need to supplement his book collection as he got to know the children in his class, and as he searched for books, he had specific children in mind. He was getting to know these children in many different ways, including gaining an understanding of them as readers and writers. He integrated his knowledge of each child with his profesional knowledge of children's literature, and this served as a guide in selecting books for the classroom.

This chapter outlines several stages of early literacy development and includes an annotated bibliography corresponding to each stage. While the list is not exhaustive, it does offer a resource for getting started in building a classroom library that supports young students' growth.

Stages of Reading Development

The annotations are categorized according to various stages of beginning reading development and/or uses in the classroom. The process of leveling books is far from exact. As a result, I hope you will use the bibliography as a general guide, subject to ongoing refinement as you observe children interacting with the books.

Keep in mind that there is no universal method for determining the level of a book or for assessing a child's level of development. However, we can offer rough descriptions of the child as a reader and descriptions of the books, including information about text structure, language, illustrations, and so on.

Trying to match a child with the right book and guiding the child's choices are critical aspects of all reading programs, regardless of the age or developing ability of the reader. Our efforts to categorize beginning reading into various stages of development are limited by considerations of the child's interests, motivation, background experience, and other factors.

How Is the List Organized?

The specific stages and accompanying descriptions have their roots in the scales of reading behavior found in *The Primary Language Record* (1988).

BOOKS FOR EMERGING READERS

These suggested books are for children who are constructing basic concepts about literacy, often labeled as "emerging literacy" in the research. This term refers to knowledge about literacy that is constructed before children come to school, but we recognize that many children build this knowledge once they actually enter school. Emerging literacy includes the development of basic concepts of print (including the concept of a word and word-by-word matching), the concept of story, book-handling skills, and the child's growing interest and pleasure in listening to stories and looking at books.

Included in this category are short books with simple text, repetitive patterns, and strong picture clues. The predictable nature of these books offers considerable support, and most can be memorized with ease. This allows the child to learn a core number of basic books by heart and gain a sense of what it feels like to be a reader (Johnston, 1992). Books in this category may also include an almost complete mapping of picture with word. These features promote a focus on the text itself and offer support for establishing the concept of word-by-word matching. The books selected for the annotated bibliography are often humorous, with the overall aim of choosing books that will engage children and inspire interest, rereading, sharing with a friend, or the desire to commit the story to memory. Many of these are also stories that children can rewrite or dictate. Finally, several selections in this category are meant to be read aloud to the children.

BOOKS FOR BEGINNING READERS-1: DEVELOPING STRATEGIES

Children at this stage understand word-by-word matching (although they may not use this concept consistently). Typically, they know a core of simple books, often by memory. These beginning readers need considerable support, as they are not yet reading with independence. However, they do

* Know a small number of words by sight

* Use some strategies for reading (children often begin by using picture clues or picture clues combined with knowledge of beginning sounds), but often rely on one strategy when reading aloud

* Often read word by word

Books for these readers are similar to those for emerging readers but generally include longer passages of text. Those listed in this annotated bibliography were selected because they have a strong story line, which allows children to make use of what is often the most natural strategy for reading: constructing meaning or sense of story.

BEGINNING READERS-2: BOOKS FOR DEVELOPING INDEPENDENCE AND PROMOTING FLUENCY

Children at this stage generally know a large core of words by sight and are using a variety of strategies for reading. These readers show greater evidence of independence; however, considerable support may still be needed. They also

* Show independence with familiar or predictable books. They need support with new and unfamiliar reading material.

* Show a growing sense of confidence

* Show greater consistency in self-monitoring and a greater integration of strategies for reading

* Often enjoy rereading familiar or favorite books

Books in this category include longer passages of text and generally require the child to use a range of strategies for reading. Vocabulary may be more difficult, but this is not always the case. Books with a strong story line are most effective as they promote the continuing development of a variety of strategies for reading and independence.

THE MODERATELY FLUENT READER

 Children at this stage are gaining increasing control over text, along with much greater independence. They

* Demonstrate greater confidence, comfort, and independence

* Can read silently for longer periods of time

* Show more independence and are more experienced with information books (nonfiction), but continue to need help with unfamiliar material

Because these readers are more fluent and more independent, the amount of reading plays an important role in developing greater fluency. At this stage, the child's independent reading experience is key: The more the child reads, the more competent and fluent he or she will become. As with any other activity (writing, playing a musical instrument, learning to swim or play tennis), practice plays an important role in developing competence and confidence. Because the moderately fluent reader can progress on his or her own by reading regularly, adults can best support the child by nurturing his or her interest and by reinforcing the child's control over text.

THE FLUENT READER

 Children at this stage are generally quite independent and experienced readers. According to *The Primary Language Record*, they

* Now approach familiar texts with confidence, but still may need support with unfamiliar material

* Often choose to read on their own (both at home and in school)

* Often choose to read silently

* Read with more focus on meaning, developing responses that show greater inferential thinking

* Show greater fluency with nonfiction and can use several sources to research a topic

Fiction

Berenstain, Stan and **Jan Berenstain,** *The Berenstain Bears and the Big Road Race,* New York: Random House, 1987.
BR-1

The Berenstain Bears are often favorites of many children, and this easy-to-read version makes them more accessible to the beginning reader. The rhyming text is predictable and offers strong picture and context clues. As the text progresses, it becomes more difficult, often requiring increased support for the child.

Other books in the First Time Readers series include: *The Berenstain Bears and the Missing Honey, The Berenstain Bears Blaze a Trail, The Berenstain Bears on the Job, The Day of the Dinosaur,* and *The Berenstain Kids: I Love Colors.*

Bonsall, Crosby, *Mine's the Best,* New York: HarperTrophy, 1973. An Early I Can Read book.
BR-1

A hot summer day at the beach provides the setting for the duel over who has the best water float. One-upmanship is the name of the game: "Mine's the best." "It is not. Mine is." "I can ride mine." "I can ride mine better." And the match continues until both floats accidentally deflate. Now the boys are more angry than ever, but an unexpected twist in the story results in their joining together as friends.

The text is simple and repetitive; the story is carried through the illustrations. This is a great book for telling the story through the pictures first, and then reading and rereading the text, which reveals the limited conversation between the two boys.

Brandenberg, Franz, *Leo and Emily,* Illustrated by Aliki, New York: Dell Young Yearling, 1981.
BR-2/MF

Young readers will delight in the adventures of Leo and Emily, who are good friends. Filled with humor and appeal, this story opens as Leo calls Emily early one morning from his apartment window—so early that it's still dark. When they meet

82

outside, they discover that getting dressed in the dark leads to all kinds of problems, such as shoes on the wrong feet and a dress that is on backward. The giggles begin slowly, ending up in belly laughs that wake up both households. This is a great book for reading alone or sharing with a friend. The text, divided into three chapters, offers the beginning reader a strong sense of story, a controlled vocabulary, and a variety of other cues. Much of the story is told through dialogue, adding to the overall readability.

There are several other books, all by the husband-and-wife team of Brandenberg and Aliki. Additional Leo and Emily titles include: *Leo and Emily's Big Ideas, Leo and Emily's Zoo, Leo and Emily and the Dragon.*

Bridwell, Norman, *The Witch Goes to School*, New York: Scholastic, 1992. Hello, Reader! series, Level 3 (grades 1 and 2).
BR-2

The everyday routine of school is turned topsy-turvy when a witch visits for the day. Magic is in the air, and each moment is filled with the unexpected.

Additional Level 3 titles include *The Blind Men and the Elephant,* and *The Fat Hat.*

Brown, Marc, *Arthur's Pet Business,* Boston: Little, Brown and Company, 1990.
MF/F

Arthur has his heart set on a new puppy. His parents say yes, but first Arthur must show them that he is responsible. This is one of many wonderful Arthur adventures.

Brown, Marc, *Pickle Things*, New York: Parents Magazine Press/Putnam and Grosset Book Group, 1980.

BR-1/BR-2

"Pickle pie and pickle cake, pickle candies and pickle shakes." These are just a few of the wild pickle things that turn up in Marc Brown's humorous rhyming verse. Picture clues, rhyme, rhythm, and repetition make this a great book for reading aloud and for the beginning reader to reread on his or her own. This book is a great springboard for reinventing one's own version of the story.

Brown, Ruth, *A Dark Dark Tale*, New York: Puffin Pied Piper, 1984.
E/BR-1

This is a variation on the familiar "In a dark dark room..."—a theme that is popular in many beginning reading books. Young readers will enjoy reading and rereading this story; the surprise ending is even more fun the second time around. Although some of the vocabulary is sophisticated, the text is simple and highly repetitive. The illustrations complement the text and add a sense of the mystery of the night.

Calmenson, Stephanie, *Roller Skates!* Illustrated by True Kelley, New York: Scholastic, 1992. Hello, Reader! series, Level 2 (K-grade 2).
BR-1/BR-2

Sam Skipper's shoe store is having a huge sale on skates and the whole town begins to ride and roll. The detailed and humorous illustrations help to tell the story and add considerable appeal. Told in rhyme, this tale will offer beginning readers a story with many available cues, including repetition, picture clues, and controlled vocabulary. Other Level 2 titles include: *All Tutus Should Be Pink; Harry Hates Shopping; Kenny and the Little Kickers; More Spaghetti, I Say; The Sword in the Stone; Two Crazy Pigs;* and *The Wrong-Way Rabbit.*

Carlson, Nancy, *I Like Me!* New York: Puffin Books, 1988.
E/B-1

Through this narrative of a perky, young pig, children have an opportunity to think about who they are, and things they like to do, and to feel good about themselves. This short, easy-to-read text has many predictable elements, including picture clues and context clues. The illustrations are lively and colorful, engaging the reader and offering strong support for the text.

Caseley, Judith, *Three Happy Birthdays.* New York: Mulberry Books, 1989.
BR-2

Benny, Marla, and Charlie the dog share each other's birthday celebration. Benny gets an umbrella. He tries out many ways to use his new present, until finally it rains! Charlie, of course, gets a bone. And Marla's present is a very special star.

These three birthday stories are told in separate chapters. The text is limited to a few lines per page, and a variety of picture and meaning clues are available to beginning readers.

Chardiet, Bernice, and **Grace Maccarone,** *The Best Teacher in the World*, Illustrated by G. Brian Karas, New York: Scholastic, 1990.
MF

Bunny can't wait to do an errand for Ms. Darcy, everyone's favorite teacher, but her excitement turns to frustration when she can't find Mrs. Walker's classroom. Afraid to show that she doesn't know the way, Bunny tells a fib and tries to fake her way through the rest of the day. An appealing story, told with warmth and humor. This book is part of Scholastic's School Friends series; other titles include: *Merry Christmas, What's Your Name?*, *Martin and the Tooth Fairy*, and *Brenda's Private Swing*.

Christian, Mary Blount, *Penrod Again*, Illustrated by Jane Dyer, New York: Aladdin Books, 1990.
BR-2

In this easy-to-read chapter book, children will enjoy the adventures of Penrod Porcupine and Griswold Bear. From spring cleaning and taking pictures with the camera, to the trauma of moving day and, finally, the joy of the Christmas season, these stories will give beginning readers a sense of confidence and success. This book is part of the Ready-to-Read series, and Mary Blount Christian has written three other titles that are part of the series: *Penrod's Pants*, *The Today and Dr. Miracle*, and *April Fool*.

Christopher, Matt, *The Dog That Pitched a No-Hitter*, Boston: Little, Brown and Company, 1988.
MF/F

This is a wonderful introduction to Matt Christopher's beloved baseball stories. In this book he tells the story of Mike and his airedale, Harry. Mike and Harry have a close relationship, so close they can read each other's minds. This comes in particularly handy as Harry likes to hang out at baseball practices. He has a knack for sizing up players on the other teams, and he doesn't forget a thing. When the big game finally arrives, Harry coaches Mike as he pitches a winning game. This is an excellent selection for children making the transition to chapter books. Children will enjoy the sequel, *The Dog That Stole Home* (1993).

Clarke, Gus, *Eddie and Teddy*, New York: Mulberry Books, 1990.
BR-2

Eddie and Teddy (his loyal stuffed bear) are best friends, and they stick side by side until Eddie goes off to school one day. Eddie is upset at first, but he soon adjusts to his new routine. Teddy is miserable, and Mom is determined to get the two back together...and they remain this way for many years to come! The book's simple text and detailed illustrations are very helpful for the beginnning reader.

Cocca-Leffler, Maryann, *What a Pest!* New York: Grosset & Dunlap, 1994. All Aboard Reading, Level 1.
E/BR-1

An appealing story about a summer at day camp and the familiar problem of the tagalong little sister. In the end, the two sisters and the friend join together and they "split a banana split." Colorful illustrations complement the text and add support for the beginning reader.

Cohen, Miriam, *Jim Meets the Thing,* Illustrated by Lillian Hoban, New York: Dell Young Yearling, 1981.
BR-2

Jim watches The Thing at home on TV. It is scary! He returns to his first-grade class the next day, embarrassed that he is the only one who was afraid of The Thing. Through an unexpected twist of events, Jim reveals his bravery to all his friends and learns that everyone is afraid of something. The story is one of several in a series about Jim and his first-grade friends. Younger readers will relate to the experiences and feelings shared in these books. Other titles include *Lost in the Museum, No Good in Art, Jim's Dog Muffins, So What?,* and *Don't Eat Too Much Turkey!*

Cohen, Miriam, *Liar, Liar, Pants on Fire!* Illustrated by Lillian Hoban, New York: Dell Young Yearling, 1985.
BR-2

Alex is new to the first-grade class, and he tries desperately to get the others to notice and accept him. Most of the children think he is telling tall tales, but Jim decides to give him another chance. Issues of honesty, friendship, and being accepted are featured.

Cole, Babette. *The Trouble with Uncle.* Boston: Little, Brown and Company, 1992.
MF

Uncle is not just an ordinary relation; he's a vibrant personality in his own right, and he's a pirate. The crazy adventure begins when he purchases a "real" treasure map and ventures off to sea. The plot thickens and each episode is more and more outlandish than the one before. Uncle ends up saving a famous movie star from the real pirates and then falling in love with a mermaid from the sea. This story is filled with comedy and the unexpected; the illustrations add to the humorous and playful tone. The text is simple; however, the vocabulary is rich and varied, adding to the complexity of the story. This book can be read aloud to children and read jointly in a shared reading context where the beginning reader receives support as needed. This book lends itself to rereading and offers a springboard to writing.

Cole, Joanna, *The Missing Tooth,* Illustrated by Marilyn Hafner, New York: Random House, 1988.
BR-2/MF

Arlo and Robby are good friends, and they share so much together, including a missing tooth in the same spot. This is a pleasing story of the ups and downs of friendship.

This text is part of Random House's Step into Reading series (this is a Step 2 book). The series has four steps and is designed to provide a range of appealing stories for children moving into literacy. Selections vary in terms of interest and appeal, so it is important to preview individual titles. Step 1 offers several easy-to-read books for children at the earliest stages of learning to read. Step 2 books are targeted for grades one to three. Step 3 books are geared toward mid-second and third grade, offering more complex text for children who are gaining independence and fluency. Step 4 books offer nonfiction titles.

Additional Step 2 recommendations include: *The Best Little Monkeys in the World*; *The Best Mistake Ever!*; *Down on the Funny Farm*; *Happy Birthday, Little Witch*; *Molly the Brave and Me*; *Monkey-Monkey's Trick*; *Pretty Good Magic*; *The Surprise Party*; and *Tom the TV Cat*.

Cushman, Doug, *Aunt Eater Loves a Mystery*, New York: HarperTrophy 1987. An I Can Read book.
BR-2

In these four chapters, children will enjoy the adventures of Aunt Eater. Each chapter involves a bit of mystery, promoting active reading and involvement in predicting what might happen next.

dePaola, Tomie, *Kit and Kat*, New York: Grosset & Dunlap, 1994. All Aboard Reading, Level 1.
E/BR-1

DePaola's colorful illustrations combine with an appealing story. The book includes three stories about the escapades of Kit and Kat, two friendly cats.

Donnelly, Liza, *Dinosaur Day*, New York: Scholastic, 1987.
BR-1

If you've ever wondered whether dinosaurs are real, you will enjoy this story. The story's narrator is sure that dinosaurs exist only in books or in the mind, until something strange happens. Although several pages contain text, most of this story is told through the illustrations. This book offers the child an opportunity to "read" the text and to create the

story through the pictures. There is a glossary of dinosaur names in the back; this may provide an enjoyable opportunity for word study for some children.

Donnelly, Liza, *Dinosaur Garden*, New York: Scholastic, 1990.
E/BR-1

A boy and his dog, Bones, contemplate what they might plant in a dinosaur garden—magnolias, pines, broccoli, and even giant asparagus. "That should attract some dinosaurs," says the boy. This is a humorous and engaging story, filled with fantasy and many special touches that invite active participation. Children will enjoy the detailed, comic book-like illustrations and the speech bubbles filled with dinosaur language. The text is simple and the illustrations perfectly complement it.

Ehlert, Lois, *Growing Vegetable Soup*, New York: Scholastic, 1987.
E/BR-1

It all begins with a few tiny seeds and some water to help them grow, and in time there will be vegetables to pick and cook for soup. Children will enjoy following the sequence from start to finish.

Large print text and colorful illustrations with labels make this a great book for beginning and emerging readers. While support will be needed, this book offers children many entry points and allows them to join in, using picture clues, sight vocabulary, and context clues. A great choice to promote interest and success.

Ehrlich, Amy, *Leo, Zack, and Emmie*, Illustrated by Steven Kellog, New York: Dial Books for Young Readers, 1981.
BR-2/MF

When Emmie Williams arrives in Miss Davis's class, Jack is intrigued. She can wiggle her ears, and she knows the names of all the dinosaurs. At first, Emmie ignores Jack's attempts to be friends, but soon, Leo, Zack, and Emmie become pals. This easy-to-read text (part of the Dial Easy-to-Read series) is broken up into four chapters that tell the continuing story of this adventurous threesome.

Engel, Diana, *Fishing*, New York: Macmillan, 1993.
MF/F

Loretta spends many quiet hours with Grandpa, waiting for a bite from the fish and enjoying their time together. When she discovers that her mother has found a new job up north, and they will be moving without Grandpa, she becomes sad, thinking that things just won't be the same. A story about a special relationship and the growth of a new friendship.

While the text is sophisticated, and support will be needed, both text and illustrations are a wonderful complement to each other. This is also an excellent story for reading aloud.

Engel, Diana, *Gino Badino*, New York: Morrow Junior Books, 1991.
MF/F

Gino spent many afternoons around the pasta factory. This gave him plenty of time to mold the dough into many wonderful creations. One day, a few of Gino's creations ended up inside the boxes of pasta to be shipped to the stores, and at last, Gino has a real job at the factory.

While much of the vocabulary is sophisticated, this is an excellent book for shared reading, and the teacher can provide support as needed.

Galdone, Paul, *The Little Red Hen*, New York: Clarion, 1973.
BR-1/BR-2

Children will enjoy reading this version of the familiar fairy tale. Prior knowledge of the story and the many predictable

features of this text will result in an enjoyable and successful experience. As always, Galdone's illustrations are inviting and a perfect complement to the text.

Galdone, Paul, *The Teeny-Tiny Woman: A Ghost Story*, New York: Clarion, 1984.
E/BR-1

Galdone has created a highly appealing version of this familiar story. With large print, repetitive text, and lively illustrations, this is an excellent book for emerging readers and beginning readers.

Galdone, Paul, *Three Aesop Fox Fables*, New York: Clarion, 1971.
MF

Readers will enjoy these three classic fox fables, accompanied by Galdone's detailed and expressive illustrations. The stories are told with simplicity and charm. This is a book that children will enjoy returning to; it could be introduced as a read-aloud, followed by informal retelling of the story. Eventually, students can take their turn at reading these tales.

Galdone, Paul, *The Three Little Pigs*, New York: Clarion, 1970.
BR-1/BR-2

This version of the familiar fairy tale has many predictable features.

Gelman, Rita Golden, *More Spaghetti, I Say!* Illustrated by Jack Kent, New York: Scholastic, 1977.
BR-1/BR-2

This repetitive, rhyming verse is sure to delight and amuse. The fun begins when Freddy invites Minnie to "Play with me, please." But Minnie is knee deep in spaghetti and ready to perform some wild and crazy antics with her much loved pasta.

Greenberg, David, *Your Dog Might Be a Werewolf, Your Toes Could All Explode,* Illustrated by George Ulrich, New York: Bantam First Skylark, 1992.
MF/F

Peter is a worrier. Will he forget to wear his clothes to school? Will he fall asleep in his soup? His brother, Frankie, is the calm one, often boasting that he has no fears, until one day Peter's worries become contagious.

The story is told in rhyming verse, which adds to the zany humor of the tale and makes this a great book for reading and rereading. The illustrations add to the humor and help capture the detail of the story.

Hill, Eric, *Spot Goes to School,* New York: Puffin, 1984.
E

The Spot books are popular with the preschool crowd, and children in kindergarten will enjoy reading these familiar books with greater independence. The text is simple, and picture clues provide considerable support. Other titles in this series include *Where's Spot?* and *Spot Goes to the Circus.*

Himmelman, John, *Simpson Snail Sings,* New York: Dutton, 1992.
MF

The adventures of Simpson the Snail are told in separate yet related stories. Whether he's telling jokes, trying to sing, or sleeping over at his friend Tucker's house, Simpson is bound to amuse and please young readers.

Hoff, Syd, *Danny and the Dinosaur,* New York: Scholastic, 1958.
BR-2

A visit to the museum winds up being quite an adventure when Danny makes friends with a dinosaur and shows him around town. The story is filled with humor and offers young children a variety of cues that will encourage risk taking and success. A strong sense of story, context clues, controlled vocabulary, and picture clues are features of this text. A classic!

Hoff, Syd, *The Horse in Harry's Room,* New York: HarperTrophy, 1970. An Early I Can Read book.
BR-1/BR-2

Harry has his very own horse in his room, but no one else can see him. This is a longtime favorite about a boy and his imaginary friend. The text is highly predictable.

Hoff, Syd, *Mrs. Brice's Mice,* New York: HarperTrophy, 1988. An Early I Can Read book.
BR-1/BR-2

Beginning readers will enjoy the humorous story of the twenty-five mice who follow in the footsteps of Mrs. Brice. Whether lifting weights or going on a supermarket shopping spree, the mice are always beside her—well, almost always. This book is filled with humor and appeal, and the surprise ending will delight young readers. This is a book children will want to share with their friends. Many cues are available, including picture clues, context and meaning clues, some repetition of sentence patterns, and a strong story line.

Impey, Rose, *The Flat Man,* Illustrated by Moira Kemp, New York: Dell Young Yearling, 1988.
MF

When it's dark and time to sleep, that's the time when the Flat Man appears. This rhythmic, rhyming verse is sure to be a crowd pleaser. Although easy to read, the language of the text is rich and complex in the images created through words. The illustrations capture the eerie and at times humorous tone of the story. This is a perfect text for rereading and reading aloud.

Kalan, Robert, *Stop Thief!* Illustrated by Yossi Abolafia, New York: Greenwillow, 1993.
BR-2

It begins slowly and innocently: A squirrel digs up the acorn that has fallen from the tree. But in an instant, another squirrel peers down from the tree, claiming the nut and accusing the first squirrel of stealing. This scene is replayed many times through, with a succession of animals all after this one little nut. Children will catch on quickly to this story's gimmick, which adds to the fun. The text is simple, highly repetitive, and predictable, resulting in a story that is very well suited for beginning readers. The illustrations are detailed and humorous and offer cues for reading the text. The style is reminiscent of Kalan's earlier book, *Jump, Frog, Jump!*

Kessler, Leonard, *Here Comes the Strikeout,* New York: HarperTrophy, 1965. An I Can Read book.
BR-2

Even Willie's lucky hat doesn't help Bobby to hit the ball and get on base. After the game, Bobby goes home feeling unhappy about all his strikeouts. With his mother's encouragement, Bobby asks Willie to work with him, and he practices every day. His hard work pays off at the next game. The text is easy to read, yet rich in content. Children will relate to Bobby's feelings and at the same time, enjoy the humorous touch.

Kessler, Leonard, *Kick, Pass, and Run,* New York: HarperTrophy, 1966. An I Can Read book.
BR-2

Kessler creates a sports favorite, filled with action and humor. Rabbit, Duck, Cat, Dog, Frog, and Owl discover a strange-looking egg in the field. It's so large that it looks like it might be a bear's egg, but they soon find out that it's a football and the game begins. Children will enjoy reading and rereading this story, which promotes beginning reading skills and develops the child's ability to use a variety of strategies for reading. The text is similar in nature to the *Old Turtle* series published by Dell Young Yearling.

Kessler, Leonard, *Old Turtle's Baseball Stories,* New York: Dell Young Yearling, 1982.
BR-2

Kessler weaves together the elements of a good story with the elements that allow beginning readers to read with independence. This collection of baseball stories is filled with action, humor, and suspense. Children will enjoy rereading this story and sharing it with friends. This text is one of several in a series about Old Turtle. Others include *Old Turtle's Soccer Team* and *Old Turtle's Winter Games.*

Koontz, Robin Michal, *Chicago and the Cat,* New York: Cobblehill Books, 1993.
MF

A quiet, snowy winter night is interrupted by an unexpected guest. Chicago, the rabbit, is not quite sure how he ended up with a kooky cat skiing through his front doorway, and he can't figure out how to get him back on the road again. Over time, the two become friends, and their adventures continue.

This story is told in four short chapters. The vocabulary is often complex, and support may be needed. This book will offer a useful transition for children who are beginning to read longer passages of text.

Krauss, Ruth, *The Carrot Seed,*
Illustrated by Crockett Johnson, New
York: HarperTrophy, 1945.
BR-2

The classic tale of a young boy who
plants a carrot seed, gives it care and attention, and waits patiently. His efforts are
rewarded.

LeSeig, Theo, *Ten Apples Up on Top,*
Illustrated by Roy McKie, New York:
Random House Beginner Books, 1961.
E/BR-1

Controlled vocabulary and strong picture clues make this counting book a popular choice for beginning readers.

Lillie, Patricia, *When This Box Is Full,*
Illustrated by Donald Crews. New York:
Greenwillow, 1993.
BR-1/BR-2

In January, as the year begins, a snow-
man's scarf is put into an empty box. As
the months pass and the seasons change,
the box is filled with a red heart, a wild
daisy, a red leaf, and much more. Crews
added color to his black-and-white photographs, resulting in illustrations that
capture detail and yet give a feeling of
fancy and fantasy.

Repetition of the months of the year and
strong correspondence between the pictures and the text make this an excellent
choice for emerging readers. The book
invites involvement from the earliest readers and offers a sense of control and success.

Lobel, Arnold, *Frog and Toad Are Friends,*
New York: HarperTrophy, 1970. An I Can
Read book.
B-2

Frog and Toad share many adventures
together, and they stick by each other
through thick and thin. Another book fea-
turing the same endearing characters is
Frog and Toad Together.

Lobel, Arnold, *Mouse Tales,* New York:
HarperTrophy, 1972. An I Can Read book.
BR-2

Papa Mouse is ready to tuck the seven
mouse boys into bed, and he has a special
treat: seven mouse tales before they go to
sleep.

Each of these stories is full of charm
and appeal. Lobel is a master storyteller,
and the simple text and vocabulary in no
way detract from his craft; rather, these elements add to the child's opportunity for a
successful independent reading experience.

Lobel, Arnold, *Owl at Home,* New York:
HarperTrophy, 1975. An I Can Read book.
BR-2

Owl settles down by the fire on a snowy
winter night, but the peaceful evening is
not meant to last. Owl hears a knock at his
door. The wind is howling, but when Owl
opens the door, no one is there. The knocking continues, and finally Owl discovers
that it is the wind knocking at his door.
When he opens the door again, winter
comes rushing into his house. This is the
first of five Owl stories that will intrigue the
reader and offer textual elements that contribute to a successful reading experience.

Lobel, Arnold, *Small Pig,* New York:
HarperTrophy, 1969. An I Can Read book.
BR-2

Small pig becomes very distressed
when the farmer and his wife decide to
clean the farm, including the pigpen. All
small pig wants is some "good, soft mud."
This strong desire leads to quite a silly
adventure, one that beginning readers are
sure to enjoy. Many cues are available to
the reader and will support success.

Lund, Jillian, *Way Out West Lives a Coyote Named Frank*, New York: Dutton, 1993.
BR-2/MF

Frank is a daring and spirited coyote who enjoys sharing a good adventure with his friends. But when all is said and done, Frank's favorite pastime is getting together with his coyote friends and creating a chorus to howl at the moon.

This story combines a rich use of language with one line of text on each page, thus offering the beginning reader an opportunity to engage in a very sophisticated reading experience. Picture clues are strong, and many easy-to-read words are included. Repetitive phrases are also included in various parts (e.g., "Once they chased a skunk, but they never did that again."). This is a perfect story for a shared experience where support can be provided as needed. The limited amount of text also makes this an excellent book for rereading, and the use of language is most appreciated when this is read aloud. The accompanying illustrations are colorful and add a tone of humor and whimsy. Children will especially enjoy the portrait of Frank with his multicolored sunglasses (also used for the cover).

Maccarone, Grace, *Itchy, Itchy Chicken Pox*, Illustrated by Betsy Lewin. New York: Scholastic, 1992. Hello Reader! series, Level 1 (preschool-grade 1).
BR-1

This personal narrative describes the all-over itches of chicken pox. The text is short and easy to read, and many cues are available to the reader, including rhyme and repetition, picture clues, and controlled vocabulary. This is one of many in the series. Other Level 1 titles include *The Bunny Hop* and *"Buzz," said the Bee*.

The Hello Reader! series is intended for beginning readers to read with their parents or independently. Each title in the series includes an introduction by consultant Priscilla Lynch, who offers several excellent suggestions for parents when they read aloud to their children or when they listen to their children read aloud.

Marshall, Edward, *Fox in Love*, Illustrated by James Marshall, New York: Puffin, 1982.
BR-2/MF

Reluctantly, Fox takes his sister, Louise, to the park, when he spots a pretty white fox on the merry-go-round. He falls madly in love. The romance has its ups and downs. In the end, Fox chooses the most unlikely dance partner of all—his sister.

This is one of several Fox books; all are part of the Puffin Easy-to-Read series. Children enjoy these stories because the controlled vocabulary, picture clues, and strong sense of story encourage success, and the stories are filled with humor. Fox is quite a character, and children love his unique approach to life.

Marshall, Edward, *Fox on Wheels*, Illustrated by James Marshall, New York: Puffin, 1983.
BR-2/MF

In these three adventures, Fox plays doctor and baby-sitter for his sister, gets up his courage to climb a tree and then realizes that getting back down is not so easy, and in the final chapter enjoys a giant race down the aisles of the supermarket. An engaging book with many predictable features.

Other Fox books in this series include *Fox at School, Fox and His Friends*, and *Fox in Love*.

Marshall, Edward, *Three by the Sea*, Illustrated by James Marshall, New York: Puffin, 1981.
BR-2

A lazy afternoon at the beach turns out

to be a bit of an adventure when Lolly, Spider, and Sam begin to tell each other stories. This is an excellent book for children who are becoming more independent and want to attempt a book on their own. The text is filled with humor and appeal. Part of the Puffin Easy-to-Read series.

Marshall, James, *Fox Be Nimble*, New York: Puffin, 1990.
BR-2/MF

Fox is up to his old tricks again. In the first story, Fox is outwitted by his three young kids, who live across the street. When Mrs. Ling asks Fox to baby-sit, he assures her he can handle them, even though he would love to be doing other things. He goes on a wild-goose chase, frantically trying to catch up with the children. In the end Fox winds up famous. In "Fox the Brave," Fox is upset when he goes roller-skating and lands on the ground with a big bang. But when Doctor Ed comes to make a house call, Fox wants to appear as brave as Louise. In "Fox on Parade," Fox stumbles over and over, trying to learn to twirl the baton, and finally he catches on, in a big way.

This is one of several Fox books. All are part of the Puffin Easy-to-Read series. Children enjoy these stories because the controlled vocabulary, picture clues and strong sense of story encourage success, and the stories are filled with humor.

Marshall, James, *Fox on the Job*, New York: Puffin, 1988.
BR-2/MF

Fox decides to show off to the girls and does a stunt on his bike. The stunt turns out to be a disaster, and the bike is a wreck. Fox asks his mother for a new bike, and his mother suggests that he get a job. Fox goes to work in the shoe store, but he winds up on the street when he tells the woman who wants "pretty little pink" shoes that

her feet are too big. Honesty is not quite the best quality for the job. Fox moves on to work at the haunted house at the amusement park, but it is much too spooky for him. Fox fares no better when he delivers pizza, but finally he finds just the right job for him. Once again, the slapstick humor should prove to be a sure winner.

Marshall, James (retold by), *Goldilocks and the Three Bears*, New York: Scholastic, 1991.
BR-2/MF

This is an updated and lively version of the familiar fairy tale. In this retelling, James Marshall reinvents the dialogue in a way that is both humorous and more realistic. Although the vocabulary and use of language are sophisticated, beginning readers have the advantage of knowing the story and will experience success with some support. This is an excellent book for follow-up role-playing and for dramatic activity.

McCully, Emily Arnold, *The Grandma Mix-Up,* New York: HarperTrophy, 1988. An I Can Read book.
BR-2

Pip's mom and dad plan a short trip away and decide to ask Pip's grandma to baby-sit. They discover a slight mix-up with the plans when both grandmas show up at the door step, each with her own idea about how things should go. One grandma is too hard, and one grandma is too easy. Finally, Pip insists that enough is enough, and he must teach them the way things are done around his house. An amusing story, told from a child's point of view.

Nagel, Karen Berman, *Two Crazy Pigs,* Illustrated by Brian Schatell, New York: Scholastic, 1992. Hello Reader! series, Level 2 (K-grade 2).
BR-1/BR-2

Mr. and Mrs. Fenster live on a farm

with two crazy pigs, whose antics drive everyone wild. This book is geared toward beginning readers who will enjoy the silly humor of the story.

O'Connor, Jane, *Eek! Stories to Make You Shriek*, Illustrated by Brian Karas, New York: Grosset and Dunlap, 1992. All Aboard Reading, Level 2 (grades 1-3).
BR-2/MF

Beginning readers will enjoy these three stories which are humorous and a bit scary at the same time. The text has many predictable features, including controlled vocabulary, picture clues, context clues, and repetitive patterns.

Parish, Peggy, *Be Ready at Eight*, Illustrated by Leonard Kessler, New York: Aladdin Books, 1979.
BR-2

Miss Molly was never very good at remembering. As hard as she tries, she can't remember why she has that little string tied around her finger.

This text is part of Aladdin's Ready-to-Read series and promotes success for beginning readers through use of controlled vocabulary, context clues, and picture clues. Peggy Parish has additional titles in this series (for example, *Granny, the Baby and the Big Gray Thing*).

Parish, Peggy, *Come Back, Amelia Bedelia*, Illustrated by Wallace Tripp, New York: HarperTrophy, 1971. An I Can Read book.
BR-2/MF

The appeal of Amelia Bedelia is well known; children of various ages take great delight in her literal interpretation of just about everything. In this story, Amelia Bedelia follows Mrs. Rogers's request for some cereal with her coffee. But a cup of coffee filled with cereal is not quite what Mrs. Rogers had in mind, and she fires Amelia Bedelia. Children will enjoy the humorous series of mishaps Amelia Bedelia encounters as she searches for another job. This book also presents a wonderful opportunity for discussion of language and figures of speech.

Parish, Peggy, *Play Ball, Amelia Bedelia*, Illustrated by Wallace Tripp, New York: HarperTrophy, 1972. An I Can Read book.
BR-2/MF

When Amelia Bedelia volunteers to fill in for one of the boys at the baseball game, the fun begins. The text allows beginning readers to make use of a variety of strategies for reading, and the strong element of humor encourages children to keep reading! A wonderful resource for motivating beginning readers to stick with it. Also in the series: *Amelia Bedelia and the Surprise Shower*, among others.

Paterson, Katherine, *The Smallest Cow in the World*, Illustrated by Jane Clark Brown, New York: HarperTrophy, 1991. An I Can Read book.
BR-2

Rosie is the meanest cow on the farm, but Marvin is crazy about her and doesn't seem to care. When he has to move away, a wave of sadness comes over him, until one day, along with the help of his imagination, Marvin figures out a way to bring Rosie back. Paterson is a master storyteller, and this one is bound to hold children's attention, promoting active involvement and interest in predicting what will happen next.

Rice, Eve, *Benny Bakes a Cake*, New York: Greenwillow, 1993.
BR-1/BR-2

This is a reissue of Rice's 1981 story about Benny's birthday and his very special birthday cake. Benny helps his mother make the cake, and everything is perfect until their dog, Ralph, decides to try some. A gentle story, geared toward preschoolers; however, the text is predictable and the vocabulary manageable for beginning readers. Children might enjoy reading this to younger brothers and sisters or to younger reading "buddies" in the school.

Rice, Eve (adapter), *Once in a Wood: Ten Tales from Aesop*, New York: Mulberry Books, 1993.
BR-2/MF

These classic Aesop fables are adapted for beginning readers in a style that promotes independence, involvement, and high interest. Rice has managed to keep these stories rich and full of appeal, and at the same time the writing is comfortable for more inexperienced readers.

This book is rich in possibilities for responses involving the arts (for example, drawing, drama, and writing).

Robins, Joan, *Addie Runs Away,* Illustrated by Sue Truesdell, New York: HarperTrophy, 1989. An Early I Can Read book.
BR-2/MF

Addie's parents want to send her to overnight camp for two weeks, but Addie worries that she will not know anyone there. Her solution? To run away. When she reconsiders this move, her friend Max and his dog, Ginger, help her get back home. Although labeled an Early I Can Read book, this text is most appropriate for a moderately fluent reader.

Rockwell, Harlow. *I Did It.* New York: Aladdin, 1974.
BR-2

In this series of six stories, each narrator describes a crafts project and how each step led to the final result. Children will enjoy learning about making masks, writing secret messages, baking bread, and

more! While the text is set up as a series of stories, it is also an excellent crafts "how-to" book. This is part of Aladdin's Ready-to-Read series.

Rockwell, Harlow, *Look at This*, New York: Aladdin, 1974.
BR-2

Similar to *I Did It*, this collection of three stories describes how to make a dancing frog, how to make applesauce, and how to make a noisemaker for New Year's Eve. Each is told in story form, but children will also enjoy using the step-by-step directions to make their own.

Rosenbloom, Joseph, *Deputy Dan Gets His Man*, Illustrated by Tim Raglin, New York: Random House, 1985.
MF

Deputy Dan is out to get the meanest man in the West—Shootin' Sam. This is a quick-paced and entertaining story of his wild escapades and comical attemps to get his man. Children will enjoy Deputy Dan, a male version of Amelia Bedelia.

This text is part of Random House's Step into Reading series (a Step 3 book). The series has four steps and is designed to provide a range of appealing stories for children who are moving into literacy.

Additional Step 3 recommendations include: *Deputy Dan and the Bank Robbers, The Little Mermaid, The Mystery of the Pirate Ghost, No Tooth, No Quarter!, Soccer Sam, Space Rock, The Titanic: Lost...and Found,* and *20,000 Baseball Cards Under the Sea.*

Rylant, Cynthia, *Henry and Mudge: The First Book*, Illustrated by Sucie Stevenson, New York: Bradbury, 1987.
MF

Henry does not have a brother or a sister, and there is no one to play with on his street. He yearns for a dog. Finally, his parents give in—they search for exactly the right companion. Lovable Mudge turns out to be a one-hundred-eighty- pound St. Bernard, and Henry and Mudge become best buddies. Although this is an excellent introduction to easy-to-read chapter books, the story is rich in style and content. Cynthia Rylant is a master storyteller.

Additional *Henry and Mudge* books include: *Henry and Mudge in Puddle Trouble, Henry and Mudge in the Green Time, Henry and Mudge Under the Yellow Moon, Henry and Mudge in the Sparkle Days,* and *Henry and Mudge and the Forever Sea.* (Note: Paperbacks published by Aladdin.)

Schwartz, Alvin, *GHOSTS! Ghostly Tales from Folklore*, Illustrated by Victoria Chess, New York: Scholastic, 1991.
BR-2/MF

This is a wonderful collection of ghost stories for the beginning reader. Although written in a straightforward, predictable style, these stories are filled with humor, mystery, and delight. There are seven individual stories, including "The Teeny-Tiny Woman" and "Ghost, Get Lost," and a catchy foreword, "Do You Believe in Ghosts?"

Schwartz, Alvin (reteller), *There Is a Carrot in My Ear and Other Noodle Tales*, Illustrated by Karen Ann Weinhaus, New York: HarperTrophy, 1982. An I Can Read book.
BR-2

"A noodle is a silly person," and in this zany collection of stories Alvin Schwartz recounts the tales of an entire "family of noodles." This book invites children to predict the hilarious outcome of each tale, encouraging active involvement and much laughter. This is a great story to share with a friend and to reread.

Sharmat, Marjorie Weinman, *Mitchell Is Moving,* Illustrated by Jose Aruego and Ariane Dewey, New York: Aladdin, 1987.
MF

Mitchell the dinosaur is tired of the same old kitchen, the same old bathroom, and the same old bedroom. He's decided to move. His neighbor Margo doesn't want to lose her dear friend's close company, and she thinks of all kinds of zany schemes to keep Mitchell around—she might even cement him to the ceiling. Filled with fun and humor, this is an enjoyable story about friendship and change. Part of the Ready-to-Read series and a Reading Rainbow Book selection, this story offers beginning readers a variety of cues.

Sharmat, Marjorie Weinman, *Nate the Great,* Illustrated by Marc Simot, New York: Dell Young Yearling, 1972.
MF

Nate the Great is the detective to top all others. In this story, Nate is in the middle of breakfast when Annie calls him on the phone to report that she lost a picture. And the adventure begins. Children will become hooked as they try to solve the case.

This is one of many in a series. This series offers the child an opportunity to read longer passages of text and provides a transition into chapter books. The series is also appealing precisely because it is one of many, and if the child enjoys it, he/she can keep reading other titles.

Other titles include: *Nate the Great Goes Undercover, Nate the Great and the Sticky Case, Nate the Great and the Snowy Trail, Nate the Great and the Lost List, Nate the Great and the Missing Key,* and *Nate the Great and the Phony Clue.*

Smith, Mavis, *A Snake Mistake,* New York: HarperCollins, 1991.
MF

Based on a true story, this is a tale

about Jake, the snake who gulped down two lightbulbs. Farmer Henry's plan to get the chickens to lay more eggs goes awry, and Jake ends up in the hospital, surrounded by a team of doctors who finally diagnose the problem. At the end of the story, there are several "Amazing Animal Activities," suggestions for readers to develop their own amazing animal story or find out more about snakes.

Stadler, John, *Hooray for Snail!,* New York: HarperTrophy, 1984.
BR-1/BR-2

Snail, in his usual slow and steady way, saves the day and the team wins the baseball game. Although the vocabulary is somewhat sophisticated, the text is simple and the pictures convey the action.

Another title is *Snail Saves the Day.*

Thaler, Mike, *A Hippopatomus Ate the Teacher,* Illustrated by Jared Lee, New York: Avon, 1981.
MF/F

A class trip to the zoo results in a wild and zany excursion when Ms. Jones falls over the rail and is swallowed up by a hippopatomus. She manages to maintain her teacherly duties; the children are escorted back to the classroom by a hippopatomus who speaks like Ms. Jones. Humorous.

Udry, Janice May, *Let's Be Enemies,* Illustrated by Maurice Sendak, New York: HarperTrophy, 1961.
B-1

James and John are very good friends, and they've shared many experiences together, including birthday parties, pretzels, umbrellas, and even the chicken pox. When James suddenly begins to show his bossy side, John is ready to poke him.

Van Leeuwen, Jean, *Tales of Oliver Pig,* Illustrated by Arnold Lobel, New York: Puffin, 1979.
B-2/MF

Children will enjoy these five stories about Oliver Pig, his younger sister Amanda and their parents. From baking cookies to a game of hide n' go seek, Oliver's adventures are familiar and often humorous.

The Puffin Easy-to-Read series is similar to HarperTrophy's I Can Read series. The books offer a strong story line, with controlled vocabulary, picture clues, and a range of available strategies.

Weiss, Nicki, *The First Night of Hannukkah,* New York: Grosset & Dunlap, 1992.
BR-2/MF

It is the first night of Hannukkah. While everyone is busy preparing for the holiday, Uncle Dan tells Molly the story of King Antiochus, the Maccabees, and the oil that kept the lights burning for eight days.

This book is part of the All Aboard Reading series (Level 2) for beginning readers.

This series offers three levels, all designed to offer the young reader a strong sense of story, controlled vocabulary, context and picture clues, and a range of appealing content. Additional titles include: *Fievel's Big Showdown* (Level 1: Preschool-Grade 1), *Ice-Cold Birthday* (Level 1), *Eek! Stories to Make You Shriek* (Level 2: Grades 1-3), *George Washington's Mother* (Level 3: Grades 2-3), and *Mike and the Magic Cookies* (Level 3).

Wells, Rosemary, *Morris's Disappearing Bag: A Christmas Story,* New York: Puffin Pied Piper/Dial, 1975.
BR-2

Wells has created a humorous and engaging story that lends itself to reading aloud, shared reading, and repeated rereadings. The illustrations are colorful and full of detail, a complement to the text and a source of support for the beginning reader. The story could also serve as a springboard to creating one's own Morris story or a Christmas story.

Wells, Rosemary, *Noisy Nora,* New York: Scholastic, 1973.
BR-1

In this humorous and engaging story, Nora the mouse is always making noise and getting into mischief. While some of the vocabulary is more sophisticated and support will be needed, this is a short, simple text with many predictable elements including strong picture clues, rhyme, and repetition.

Wiseman, B., *Morris the Moose,* New York: HarperTrophy, 1989. An Early I Can Read book.
BR-1/BR-2

Morris is sure that the cow he meets along the road is a moose. Why, of course!—he has four legs and a tail. Morris earnestly tries to convince him, drawing a deer and a horse into the controversy. After considerable banter back and forth, Morris finally realizes that he made a "MOOSEtake." Simple text, repetitive patterns, and a strong story line will support beginnning readers. Children will enjoy the silly humor.

Ziefert, Harriet, *Nicky, 1-2-3,* Illustrated by Richard Brown, New York: Puffin, 1995.
E/BR-1

This text is part of the Lift-the Flap series, a useful addition to kindergarten and first-grade classrooms. The books are highly repetitive, with simple text and lift-up flaps that invite active involvement. This text develops counting skills and knowledge about animals and their babies.

Other titles in the series include: *Don't Cry Baby Sam, Nicky's Christmas Surprise; Nicky's Noisy Night; Nicky's Picnic; Oh No, Nicky!;* and *What's Polite?*

Ziefert, James, *Harry Goes to Day Camp,* Illustrated by Mavis Smith, New York: Puffin, 1990.
BR-1/BR-2

The bus ride to camp is filled with anticipation and many voices joining in song. Harry is excited, but the thing he really wants to do the most is swim. This text is part of the Hello Reading! series, an excellent resource for beginning readers. Humorous and highly predictable, offering children controlled vocabulary, repetition, colorful illustrations and picture clues, and a strong sense of story.

Zion, Gene, *Harry and the Lady Next Door,* Illustrated by Margaret Bloy Graham, New York: HarperTrophy, 1960. An Early I Can Read book.
BR-2

This is one of several books about Harry, a friendly white dog with black spots. In this story, Harry struggles to find a way to get the lady next door to stop singing. Highly predictable and engaging!

Nonfiction

In general, nonfiction books tend to be more sophisticated and complex than fiction. In addition, the purposes for reading nonfiction are often quite different than for fiction. It is important to guide children in understanding these differences and to help them develop strategies for reading nonfiction.

The nonfiction titles in this list are generally for the moderately fluent and fluent reader. Quite often, even more independent readers will require additional support for reading and understanding the structure of the text. With support, though, all children will enjoy reading these books (labeled **AS/MF**).

These books can be used in a variety of different ways, depending upon the purpose for reading. For example, children at the earliest stages might preview the illustrations and read captions and labels that correspond with these pictures. A more fluent reader might select the same text, reading more of the detailed information in the body of the text. Many of the more recent nonfiction publications offer a varied and lively format, thus appealing to children of different ages and abilities.

In some cases, when a book is appropriate for independent reading, a stage of development is indicated in bold print.

Barrett, N.S., *Monkeys and Apes*, New York: Franklin Watts, 1988.
AS/MF

This book is part of the Picture Library series, a collection of visual reference books that combine color photos with information about a variety of topics. Titles include books about animals (*Bears, Big Cats, Monkeys and Apes*, and *Pandas*); about sports vehicles (*Canoeing, Custom Cars, Race Cars, Trail Bikes*); about recreational vehicles (*Airliners, Helicopters, Motorcycles*, and *Trucks*); and about military vehicles (*Aircraft Carriers, Submarines*, and *Tanks*). Text layout is varied and appealing; however, adult support will be required.

Barton, Byron, *Building a House*, New York: Mulberry, 1981.
BR-2

In this picture book, children can discover the step-by-step process of building a house. From digging the hole in the ground and pouring the cement for the foundation to the final stages of plumbing, electrical work, and painting, this book gives a sim-

ple yet detailed insight into building. The colorful illustrations complement the text and offer additional support to the beginning reader.

Brennan, Frank, *Reptiles*, Illustrated by Malcolm Livingstone, New York: Aladdin, 1992.
AS/MF

This text is part of Aladdin's BASICS series, a collection of nonfiction books designed to introduce children to the basics of the world around them. Titles include *Creepy Crawlies, Out in Space, Under the Sea, What Do I Eat?, And Now...The Weather, What Am I Made Of?*, and *Our Planet Earth*. Adult support will be required to read the text, but the colorful watercolor illustrations invite curious young readers to learn on their own.

Clutton-Brock, Juliet, *Dog*. New York: Alfred A. Knopf, 1991.
AS/MF

This text is part of the Eyewitness series, a popular collection of nonfiction books known for its appealing mix of color photography and varied layout, attracting readers of all degrees of fluency. This series was first published in London by Dorling Kindersley Limited. Other titles include *Ancient Egypt, Arms and Armor, Bird, Car, Cat, Explorer, Fossil, Invention, Mammal, Music, Reptile, Rocks and Minerals, Shells*, and *Weather*.

Florian, Douglas, *A Chef*, New York: Greenwillow, 1992.
AS/MF

Florian gives us a firsthand view of a typical day in the life of a chef. She begins her day early in the morning, shopping for food and planning the menu. The illustrations and the text show each step of the day, from food preparation and cooking to serving customers in restaurants, schools and many other places where people eat.

This book is part of the How We Work series. Other titles include *An Auto Mechanic, A Carpenter, A Potter,* and *A Painter.*

Florian, Douglas, *City Street,* New York: Greenwillow, 1990.
AS/MF

Florian's colorful and lively illustrations combine with rhyming text to create a portrait of city life. From "City street, Jumping feet" to "Twilight and "City night," children will enjoy the way illustrations and text work together, inviting active involvement on the part of the reader. This is an excellent introduction to nonfiction. Florian invites the beginning reader to begin using a variety of strategies for reading, combining prior experience with picture clues, beginning sounds, and rhyming words.

Gay, Tanner Ottley, *Sharks in Action,* Illustrated by Jean Cassels, New York: Aladdin, 1990.
AS/MF

Even emerging readers will enjoy the learning through the pop-ups and accompanying captions. This book is engaging and appealing for readers at various stages of reading development.

Heinst, Marie, *My First Number Book,* New York: Dorling Kindersley, 1992.
AS/MF

Basic number concepts are introduced through a series of colorful photographs and engaging questions and activities. Designed for shared reading, this book encourages conversation between parent and child, and teacher and child, or among small groups of children. The bright color photos depicting many familiar objects and activities will lure children into discussion and careful study of each page.

The layout and design promotes reading of the major headings and various labels that accompany many of the photographs. This is a book children will want to return to again and again.

Jeunesse, Gallimard and **Pascale de Bourgoing,** *The Egg,* Illustrated by Rene Mettler, New York: Scholastic, 1989.
AS/MF

This book tracks the development of a young chick from the time the hen sits on her eggs to keep them warm to the moment the egg hatches. Young readers will also learn about other animals who lay eggs. Colorful and detailed illustrations and transparencies coordinate with the text. This is a very accessible nonfiction selection for beginning readers.

This is part of the First Discovery Book series. Other titles include: *Airplanes, Bears, Cats, Colors, The Earth and Sky, The Tree, Fruit, The Ladybug,* and *Weather.*

Ling, Mary, *Calf,* Photographed by Gordon Clayton, New York: Dorling Kindersley, 1993.
AS/MF

Told from the baby calf's perspective, this story traces the growth cycle of the calf. Color photographs illustrate the development showing various aspects of the young calf's life, including grazing in the meadow, milking, and the passage into motherhood.

This book is part of the See How They Grow series. Other titles include *Butterfly, Foal, Fox, Giraffe, Penguin, Pig, Owl, Puppy, Kitten, Frog, Duck, Lamb, Rabbit, Chick,* and *Mouse.* While beginning and emerging readers will need support with the text, the layout and design encourage active involvement. The detailed photographs and simple headings with limited text allow the child to make sense of the story.

Micklethwait, Lucy (selector), *I Spy Two Eyes: Numbers in Art*, New York: Greenwillow, 1993.
AS/MF

This gamelike approach to great works of art will engage readers in close observation of individual paintings. Artists include Gauguin, Matisse, Kandinsky, van Gogh, Picasso, Botticelli, Rubens, and Rousseau. The "I Spy" approach offers repetition, simple text, and strong picture clues for beginning readers.

Parker, Steve, *Human Body: Investigate and Understand Your Amazing Body,* New York: Dorling Kindersley, 1994.
AS/MF

This pocket-sized book explores all aspects of the human body, including appearance, skin, hair and nails, muscles, bones, the heart, blood, the lungs and breathing, food, teeth, the brain, and more! While the text is more difficult and support will be needed, the layout and design are highly engaging and offer young readers opportunities to read the labels, questions, and short passages of text.

This book is part of the Eyewitness Explorers series; other titles include *Weather, Birds, Flowers, Insects, Shells, Rocks and Minerals,* and *Seashore.*

Rockwell, Anne and **Harlow Rockwell,** *Machines,* New York: HarperTrophy, 1972.
E/BR-1

This picture book describes levers, wheels, pulleys, ball bearings, gears, and more!

Rockwell, Harlow, *I Did It,* New York: Aladdin Books, 1974.
BR-2

In this series of six stories, each narrator describes a crafts project and how each step led to the final result. Children will enjoy learning about making masks, writing secret messages, baking bread, and more! While the text is set up as a series of stories, it is also an excellent crafts "how-to" book. This is part of Aladdin's Read-to-Read series.

Rockwell, Harlow, *Look at This,* New York: Aladdin, 1974.
BR-2

Similar to *I Did It*, this collection of three stories describes how to make a dancing frog, how to make applesauce, and how to make a noisemaker for New Year's Eve. Each is told in story form, but children will also enjoy using the step-by-step directions to do their own creations. This is part of Aladdin's Ready-to-Read series.

Royston, Angel, *Sea Animals,* Photography by Steve Shott, New York: Aladdin, 1992.
AS/MF

Bright color photographs and text combine in this description of various sea animals. Children will learn about crabs, dolphins, clownfish, sea lions, starfish, and more in this lively and appealing book. The text is limited, and while adult support will be required for the actual reading, this series is a perfect introduction to nonfiction.

This text is part of the Eye-Openers series (originally published in London by Dorling Kindersley Limited); other titles include *Baby Animals, Farm Animals, Zoo Animals, Trucks, Pets, Diggers and Dump Trucks, Dinosaurs, Jungle Animals, Cars,* and *Planes.*

Royston, Angela, *Ships and Boats,* Photography by Steve Shott, New York: Aladdin, 1992.
AS/MF

In this text, children are introduced to sailboats, motorboats, cruise ships, fishing boats, and a variety of other boats and ships. Each page includes a colorful photograph of the boat, drawings showing the parts of the boat, and a short description of the boat in action. Support will be needed for the narrative descriptions; however, early readers will quickly read the various labels that accompany the photos and drawings.

This is part of the Eye-Openers Series. Other titles: *Baby Animals, Zoo Animals, Jungle Animals, Pets, Dinosaurs, Cars, Trucks,* and *Planes.*

Taylor, Barbara, *Rain Forest: A Close-Up Look at the Natural World of a Rain Forest,* Photographs by Frank Greenway, New York: Dorling Kindersley, 1992.
AS/MF

In the lush, shady world of the rain forest, we meet a host of wildlife, including a frog, a postman caterpillar, a postman butterfly, a fruit bat, hairy spiders, and deadly orchids. Each page is more alluring than the next, with detailed color photographs inviting close study. This is a book that will stimulate many questions and great conversation, and perhaps provide a springboard for further reading, research, and writing.

The layout includes labels, captions, brief descriptions, and longer passages of text. It is diverse, offering opportunities for detailed, extensive reading or more casual reading of shorter sections.

This book is part of the Look Closer series; other titles include *Cave Life, Coral Reef, Desert Life, Forest Life, Meadow Life, Pond Life, River Life, Shoreline, Swamp Life, Tide Pool,* and *Tree Life.*

von Noorden, Djinn (editor), *The Lifesize Animal Counting Book,* New York: Dorling Kindersley, 1994.
AS/MF

Lively color photographs invite young children to count and read along. This is an enormously engaging counting book that lends itself to a variety of reading situations. It is perfect for sharing between parent and child and teacher and child, among small groups of children, or for independent reading. Whether counting five wise owls, three playful puppies, or nine nosy guinea pigs, this book involves children in counting and exploring the sounds of language.

Ziefert, Harriet, *Let's Get a Pet,* Illustrated by Mavis Smith, New York: Viking, 1993.
AS/MF

Filled with humor and situations that children can relate to, this informational book focuses on how to pick the right pet. The text includes a discussion of making the decision as a family, taking care of a pet, and specific information about small furry animals, birds, fish, cats, and dogs.

Ziefert, Harriet, *Under the Water,* Illustrated by Suzy Mandel, New York: Puffin, 1990.
BR-2/MF

Informative text and detailed, colorful illustrations tell about sea life. A wonderful introduction to nonfiction.

Humor/Joke Books/ Wordplay

Most of all, let your students have fun with these books. Whether it's knock-knock jokes or tongue twisters, there is no better way to encourage reading than through laughter.

Please note that some of the books are more difficult and would require a more fluent reader to read independently. However, the intent is for youngsters to read these books with adult support (**AS/MF**).

Offer your guidance and the children will respond in kind.

Cole, Joanna, and **Stephanie Calmenson,** *Six Sick Sheep: 101 Tongue Twisters,* Illustrated by Alan Tiegreen, New York: Beech Tree, 1993.
MF

An appealing and humorous collection with many familiar tongue twisters, such as "How much wood would a woodchuck chuck?" and "Betty Botter bought some butter," as well as some new twists on words. This is an excellent resource for whole-class or small-group sessions in which beginning sounds are reviewed.

Cole, Joanna, and **Stephanie Calmenson,** *Yours Till Banana Splits: 201 Autograph Rhymes,* Illustrated by Alan Tiegreen, New York: Beech Tree, 1995.
MF

Cole and Calmenson spent hours reading through their friends' old autograph albums, enjoying rhymes that brought back memories of good times and friendships. The results of their research are in this collection of rhymes, which are sure to invite laughter and an interest in playing with language.

Folsom, Marcia, and **Michael Folsom,** *Easy as Pie: A Guessing Game of Sayings,* Illustrated by Jack Kent, New York: Clarion, 1985.
AS/MF

With a touch of humor and zaniness, this book combines speech play with a guessing game that is sure to engage beginning readers. From "straight as an arrow" to "silly as a goose," this text includes old and new comparisons. The book encourages children to play with language and make up their own sayings. Beginning readers can make use of a variety of strategies, including alphabetical order, picture

clues, rhymes, and prior experience with familiar sayings and figures of speech.

Hall, Katy, and **Lisa Eisenberg,** *Buggy Riddles,* Illustrated by Simms Taback, New York: Puffin, 1986. Puffin Easy-to-Read.
MF

A collection of riddles that is sure to arouse laughter and interest. Children will enjoy sharing these riddles with a friend or reading them on their own, and the positive experience will invite rereading. The cartoonlike illustrations are colorful, detailed, and very funny. Although the vocabulary is sophisticated, the format is simple and easy to follow, and the amount of text per page is limited, making this an inviting book for children at earlier stages of reading development. With support, this book can be used with emerging, beginning, and more-fluent readers.

Hall, Katy and **Lisa Eisenberg,** *Grizzly Riddles,* Illustrated by Nicole Rubel, New York: Puffin, 1989. Puffin Easy-to-Read.
MF

"Why didn't the grizzly walk on the gravel road? She had bear feet!" This is just a taste of the many wonderful bear riddles and puns in this witty, zany, and appealing book. Colorful illustrations. A great follow-up to *Buggy Riddles.*

Hartman, Victoria, *The Silliest Joke Book Ever,* Illustrated by R.W. Alley, New York: Lothrop, Lee & Shepard Books, 1993.
AS/MF

This collection of zany riddles and jokes is organized by topic. There are jokes about animals, food, travel, monsters, and other gruesome folks, and even a contemporary set of "Techie Ticklers."

Hawkins, Colin, and **Jacqui Hawkins,** *Knock! Knock!* New York: Aladdin, 1991.
BR-2/MF

This book of knock-knock jokes is in pop-up form, inviting children to interact with the text and illustrations. The layout is sometimes difficult to follow, and support may be needed the first time through, but this is a book that children will want to read over and over. Each page is alive with words and pictures, and the jokes will engage children in active play with language.

Keller, Charles, *Belly Laughs: Food Jokes and Riddles*, Illustrated by Ron Fritz, New York: Simon and Schuster, 1990.
MF/F

"Where do burgers dance? At the meat ball." "What do ants use for hula hoops? Cheerios." This collection of food jokes and riddles will amuse young listeners and invite them to reread their favorites.

Keller, Charles, *Tongue Twisters,* Illustrated by Ron Fritz, New York: Simon and Schuster, 1989.
AS/MF

Several of these tongue twisters are old favorites that children will know; others offer new challenges for reading aloud. This book is perfect for sharing with a small or large group, reading aloud, and rereading many times. Because tongue twisters are meant to be reread, they offer a context for developing basic strategies, such as word-by-word matching, beginning sounds, blends, and rhyming words.

Kessler, Leonard, *Old Turtle's 90 Knock-Knocks, Jokes, and Riddles*, New York: Mulberry, 1991.
BR-2/MF

Fans of Kessler's sports tales (for example, *Old Turtle's Baseball Stories, Old Turtle's Winter Games*, etc.) are sure to enjoy these knock-knocks, jokes, and riddles. The collection uses controlled vocabulary, making this a relatively easy-to-read joke book and excellent for independent reading. Each one of Old Turtle's friends has a section of his own jokes.

Rayner, Shoo, *My First Picture Joke Book*, New York: Picture Puffins, 1991.
MF

"What is black and white and has sixteen wheels? A zebra on roller skates." These and many more jokes are accompanied by detailed illustrations that capture the essence of each. Although the vocabulary is sophisticated, the text is simple and the pictures provide an important aid for the young reader.

Schwartz, Alvin, *Ten Copycats in a Boat and Other Riddles*, New York: HarperTrophy, 1980. An I Can Read book.
BR-1/BR-2

"Ten copycats were sitting in a boat, and one jumped out. How many were left?" Familiar riddles like this and some zany new ones are combined into this humorous book. Children will enjoy the punch lines and become engaged in the guessing game.

Schwartz, Alvin (reteller), *There is a Carrot in My Ear and Other Noodle Tales*, Illustrated by Karen Ann Weinhaus, New York: HarperTrophy, 1982. An I Can Read book.
BR-2

"A noodle is a silly person," and in this zany collection of stories, Alvin Schwartz recounts the tales of an entire "family of noodles." This book invites children to predict the hilarious outcome of each tale, encouraging active involvement and much laughter.

Poetry

Through poetry, children explore the sounds and richness of language and language play. Books in this genre offer many possibilities for helping kids enjoy poetry and build skills and strategies for reading.

The poetry books in this section can be used in many ways with a variety of readers. A teacher might read poetry aloud, followed by a choral reading experience and/or children rereading on their own. Children might be asked to reinvent their own version of the poem and read their version.

Titles that list a categorization according to stage of reading development can be read with greater independence; those titles (labeled **AS/MF**) are more complex and sophisticated and should be used with adult support. In all cases, these collections contain poems that beginning readers can read on their own, with a sense of joy and accomplishment.

Benjamin, Alan, *A Nickel Buys a Rhyme,* Illustrated by Karen Lee Schmidt, New York: Morrow Junior, 1993.
AS/MF

> What's for Lunch?
> A spider invited
> a fly for lunch.
> Crunch.
> Crunch.
> Crunch.

This is a collection of rhymes filled with humor and animation. Children will enjoy the playful tone and engaging nature of these poems.

These rhymes are perfect for reading aloud, for choral reading, and for rereading.

Brown, Marc, *Pickle Things,* New York: Parents Magazine Press/Putnam & Grosset, 1980.
BR-1/BR-2

"Pickle pie and pickle cake, pickle candies and pickle shakes." These are just a few of the wild pickle things that turn up in Marc Brown's humorous rhyming verse. Picture clues, rhyme, rhythm, and repetition make this a great book for reading aloud and for the beginning reader to reread on his or her own. This book is a great springboard for reinventing one's own version of the story.

Cole, Joanna, and **Stephanie Calmenson,** *Yours Till Banana Splits: 201 Autograph Rhymes,* Illustrated by Alan Tiegreen, New York: Beech Tree, 1995.
MF

Cole and Calmenson spent hours reading through their friends' old autograph albums, enjoying rhymes that brought back memories of good times and friendships. The results of their research are in this collection of rhymes, which are sure to invite laughter and an interest in playing with language. This is a book that will invite rereading and perhaps some writing, too. An excellent addition to any classroom library.

Florian, Douglas, *Bing Bang Boing,* New York: Harcourt Brace & Company, 1994.
AS/MF

Florian's poems will delight and amuse; all are great for reading aloud. Many of these poems will also be appealing to beginning readers. With some opportunity for demonstration and rehearsal (perhaps through choral reading), children will enjoy rereading some of the easier poems on their own.

Goldstein, Bobbye S. (selector), *What's On the Menu?* Illustrated by Chris L. Demarest, New York: Viking, 1992.
AS/MF

This is a collection of poems about food and the art of eating. Goldstein's selections are full of humor and include many of children's favorite poets, such as Jack Prelutsky, Eve Merriam, Lee Bennett Hopkins, Myra Cohn Livingston, and Arnold Adoff.

Hopkins, Lee Bennett (selector), *Munching: Poems About Eating*, Boston: Little, Brown, 1985.
AS/MF

Lee Bennett Hopkins has selected a myriad of poems that are sheer delight and that will inspire children to share them with their friends. He brings us a collection that includes Jack Prelutsky, Arnold Adoff, Russell Hoban, Lewis Carroll, Ogden Nash, and Steven Kroll.

Parry, Caroline, *Zoomerang a Boomerang: Poems to Make Your Belly Laugh*, Illustrated by Michael Martchenk, New York: Puffin Books, 1993.
BR-2/MF

This book contains several traditional poems and songs (for example, "Kookaburra," "Head and Shoulders") and many newer poems designed to delight and amuse. The controlled vocabulary and limited text make this a very appealing book for beginning readers. The poems invite smiles, participation, and rereading. This collection will be appealing and instructional for children at various stages of beginning reading.

Prelutsky, Jack (selector), *Poems of A. Nonny Mouse*, Illustrated by Henrik Drescher, New York: Dragonfly/Alfred A. Knopf, 1989.
AS/MF

This collection is filled with all that is exaggerated, silly, and absurd. Great for reading aloud to children, this is also a book that they will want to return to on their own. There are poems that are appropriate for the various stages of beginning reading development.

Prelutsky, Jack, *The New Kid on the Block,* Illustrated by James Stevenson, New York: Greenwillow, 1984.

From alligators to itches, this collection is sure to invite active involvement and laughter. Another Prelutsky favorite that is sure to amuse and engage children.

Prelutsky, Jack, *Rolling Harvey Down the Hill,* Illustrated by Victoria Chess, New York: Mulberry, 1993.
MF

Using a blend of humor and rhyming verse, Prelutsky tells the adventures of Tony, Lumpy, Harvey, and Will. These four friends experience a bit of everything, from fighting with each other or getting into some sort of trouble to playing practical jokes or rolling Harvey down the hill. Another Prelutsky favorite!

Prelutsky, Jack, *Something Big Has Been Here,* Illustrated by James Stevenson, New York: Greenwillow, 1990.
AS/MF

Prelutsky's poems are sure winners, and children will become actively involved in sharing the poems. This collection can be a wonderful springboard for children writing their own poems (individually, in small groups, or as a whole-class, teacher-guided activity). These poems provide another wonderful source of text for reading aloud.

Schwartz, Alvin, *I Saw You in the Bathtub and Other Folk Rhymes,* Illustrated by Syd Hoff, New York: HarperTrophy, 1989.
An I Can Read book.
BR-2

This is a collection of numerous folk rhymes, including many familiar favorites and new surprises that are sure to delight and amuse. The zany humor should appeal to young readers.

Silverstein, Shel, *A Light in the Attic,*
New York: Harper & Row, 1981.
AS/MF

This collection is great for reading aloud, and for rereading. While the vocabulary and use of language is often sophisticated, many of the poems will engage beginning readers in listening and then reading these poems on their own. Silverstein uses his imagination to explore a wide range of topics, including messy rooms, a rock 'n' roll band, frisbees, homework, and even getting dressed but having that awful feeling that something is missing.

By Author

Barrett, N.S.
Monkeys and Apes.
New York: Franklin
Watts, 1988.
AS/MF

Barton, Bryon.
Building a House.
New York: Mulberry,
1981.
BR-2

Benjamin, Alan.
Illus. by Karen Lee
Schmidt.
A Nickel Buys a Rhyme.
New York: Morrow
Junior, 1993.
AS/MF

**Berenstain, Stan and Jan
Berenstain.**
*The Berenstain Bears
and the Big Road Race.*
New York: Random
House, 1987.
BR-1

Bonsall, Crosby.
Mine's the Best.
New York:
HarperTrophy, 1973. An
Early I Can Read book.
BR-1

Brandenberg, Franz.
Illus. by Aliki.
Leo and Emily.
New York: Dell Young
Yearling, 1981.
BR-2/MF

Brennan, Frank.
Illus. by Malcolm
Livingstone.
Reptiles.

New York: Aladdin,
1992.
AS/MF

Bridwell, Norman.
*The Witch Goes to
School.*
New York: Scholastic,
1992.
Hello Reader! series,
Level 3 (Grade 1 and 2)
BR-2

Brown, Marc.
Arthur's Pet Business.
Boston: Little, Brown
and Company, 1990
MF/F

Brown, Marc.
Pickle Things.
New York: Parents
Magazine Press/Putnam
& Grosset Book Group,
1980.
BR-1/BR-2

Brown, Ruth.
A Dark Dark Tale.
New York: Puffin Pied
Piper, 1984.
E/BR-1

Calmenson, Stephanie.
Illus. by True Kelley
Roller Skates!
New York: Scholastic,
1992.
Hello Reader! series,
Level 2 (K-Grade 2).
BR-1/BR-2

Carlson, Nancy.
I Like Me!
New York: Puffin Books,
1988.
E/B-1

Caseley, Judith.
Three Happy Birthdays.
New York: Mulberry
Books,1989.
BR-2

**Chardiet, Bernice, and
Grace Maccarone.**
Illus. by G. Brian Karas.
*The Best Teacher in the
World.*
New York: Scholastic,
1990.
MF

Christian, Mary Blount.
Illus. by Jane Dyer.
Penrod Again.
New York: Aladdin
Books, 1990.
BR-2

Christopher, Matt.
*The Dog That Pitched a
No-Hitter.*
Boston: Little, Brown
and Company, 1988.
MF/F

Clarke, Gus.
Eddie and Teddy.
New York: Mulberry
Books, 1990.
BR-2

Clutton-Brock, Juliet.
Dog.
New York: Alfred A.
Knopf, 1991.
AS/MF

Cocca-Leffler, Maryann.
What a Pest!
New York: Grosset &
Dunlap, 1994.
All Aboard Reading,
Level 1.
E/BR-1

Cohen, Miriam.
Illus. by Lillian Hoban.
Jim Meets the Thing.
New York: Dell Young
Yearling, 1981.
BR-2

Cohen, Miriam.
Illus. by Lillian Hoban.
Liar, Liar, Pants on Fire!
New York: Dell Young
Yearling, 1985.
BR-2

Cole, Babette.
The Trouble with Uncle.
Boston: Little, Brown
and Company, 1992.
MF

Cole, Joanna and
Stephanie Calmenson.
Illus. by Alan Tiegreen.
*Six Sick Sheep: 101
Tongue Twisters.*
New York: Beech Tree,
1993.
MF

Cole, Joanna and
Stephanie Calmenson.
Illus. by Alan Tiegreen.
*Yours Till Banana Splits:
201 Autograph Rhymes.*
New York: Beech Tree,
1995.
MF

**Cole, Joanna and
Stephanie Calmenson.**
Illus. by Alan Tiegreen.
Yours Till Banana Splits:

201 Autograph Rhymes.
New York: Beech Tree,
1995.
MF

Cole, Joanna.
Illus. by Marilyn Hafner.
The Missing Tooth.
New York: Random
House, 1988.
BR-2/MF

Cushman, Doug.
*Aunt Eater Loves a
Mystery.*
New York:
HarperTrophy 1987.
An I Can Read book.
BR-2

dePaola, Tomie.
Kit and Kat.
New York: Grosset and
Dunlap, 1994.
All Aboard Reading,
Level 1.
E/BR-1

Donnelly, Liza.
Dinosaur Day.
New York: Scholastic,
1987.
BR-1

Donnelly, Liza.
Dinosaur Garden.
New York: Scholastic,
1990.
E/BR-1

Ehlert, Lois.
*Growing Vegetable
Soup.*
New York: Scholastic,
1987.
E/BR-1

Ehrlich, Amy.
Illus. by Steven Kellog.
Leo, Zack, and Emmie.
New York: Dial Books

for Young Readers, 1981.
BR-2/MF

Engel, Diana.
Fishing.
New York: Macmillan,
1993.
MF/F

Engel, Diana.
Gino Badino.
New York: Morrow
Junior Books, 1991.
MF/F

Florian, Douglas.
A Chef.
New York:
Greenwillow, 1992.
AS/MF

Florian, Douglas.
City Street.
New York:
Greenwillow, 1990.
AS/MF

Florian, Douglas.
Bing Bang Boing.
New York: Harcourt
Brace & Company, 1994.
AS/MF

Folsom, Marcia, and
Michael Folsom.
Illus. by Jack Kent.
*Easy as Pie : A Guessing
Game of Saying.*
New York: Clarion,
1985.
AS/MF

Galdone, Paul.
The Little Red Hen.
New York: Clarion,
1973.
BR-1/BR-2

Galdone, Paul.
The Teeny-Tiny Woman: A Ghost Story.
New York: Clarion, 1984.
E/BR-1

Galdone, Paul.
The Three Little Pigs.
New York: Clarion, 1970.
BR-1/BR-2

Galdone, Paul.
Three Aesop Fox Fables.
New York: Clarion, 1971.
MF

Gay, Tanner Ottley.
Illus. by Jean Cassels.
Sharks in Action
New York: Aladdin, 1990.
AS/MF

Gelman, Rita Golden.
Illus. by Jack Kent.
More Spaghetti, I Say!
New York: Scholastic, 1977.
BR-1/BR-2

Goldstein, Bobbye S.
(selector).
Illus. by Chris L. Demarest.
What's On the Menu?
New York: Viking, 1992.
AS/MF

Greenberg, David.
Illus. by George Ulrich.
Your Dog Might Be a Werewolf, Your Toes Could All Explode.
New York: Bantam First Skylark, 1992.
MF/F

Hall, Katy and Lisa Eisenberg.
Illus. by Simms Taback.
Buggy Riddles.
New York: Puffin, 1986.
Easy-to-Read.
MF

Hall, Katy and **Lisa Eisenberg.**
Illus. by Nicole Rubel.
Grizzy Riddles.
New York: Puffin, 1989.
Puffin Easy to read.
MF

Hartman, Victoria.
Illus. by R.W. Alley.n
The Silliest Joke Book Ever.
New York: Lothrop, Lee & Shepard Books, 1993.
AS/MF

Hawkins, Colin and **Jacqui Hawkins.**
Knock! Knock!
New York: Aladdin, 1991.
BR-2/MF

Heinst, Marie.
My First Number Book.
New York: Dorling Kindersley, 1992.
AS/MF

Hill, Eric.
Spot Goes to School.
New York: Puffin, 1984.
E

Himmelman, John.
Simpson Snail Sings.
New York: Dutton, 1992.
MF

Hoff, Syd.
Danny and the Dinosaur.
New York: Scholastic, 1958.
BR-2

Hoff, Syd.
Mrs. Brice's Mice.
New York: HarperTrophy, 1988.
An Early I Can Read Book
BR-1/BR-2

Hoff, Syd.
The Horse in Harry's Room.
New York: HarperTrophy (An Early I Can Read Book), 1970.
BR-1/BR-2

Hopkins, Lee Bennett (Selector).
Munching Poems about Eating.
Boston: Little, Brown, 1985.
AS/MF

Impey, Rose.
Illus. by Moira Kemp.
The Flat Man.
New York: Dell Young Yearling, 1988.
MF

Jeunesse, Gallimard and **Pascale de Bourgoing.**
Illus. by Rene Mettler.
The Egg.
New York: Scholastic, 1989.
AS/MF

Kalan, Robert.
Illus. by Yossi Abolafia.
Stop Thief!
New York: Greenwillow, 1993.
BR-2

Keller, Charles.
illlus. by Ron Fritz.
*Belly Laughs: Food
Jokes and Riddles.*
New York: Simon &
Schuster, 1990.
MF/F

Keller, Charles.
Illus. by Ron Fritz.
Tongue Twisters.
New York: Simon &
Schuster, 1989.
AS/MF

Kessler, Leonard.
*Here Comes the
Strikeout.*
New York:
HarperTrophy, 1965. An
I Can Read book.
BR-2

Kessler, Leonard.
Kick, Pass, and Run.
New York:
HarperTrophy, 1966. An
I Can Read book.
BR-2

Kessler, Leonard.
*Old Turtle's Baseball
Stories.*
New York: Dell Young
Yearling, 1982.
BR-2

Kessler, Leonard.
*Old Turtle's 90 Knock-
Knocks, Jokes, and
Riddles.*
New York: Mulberry,
1991.
BR-2/MF

Koontz, Robin Michal.
Chicago and the Cat.
New York: Cobblehill
Books, 1993.
MF

Krauss, Ruth.
Illus. by Crockett
Johnson.
The Carrot Seed.
New York:
HarperCollins, 1945.
BR-2

LeSeig, Theo.
Illus. by Roy McKie.
Ten Apples Up on Top.
New York: Random
House Beginner Books,
1961.
E/BR-1

Lillie, Patricia.
Illus. by Donald Crews.
When This Box Is Full.
New York:
Greenwillow, 1993.
BR-1/BR-2

Ling, Mary.
photographed by Gordon
Clayton.
Calf.
New York: Dorling
Kindersley, 1993.
AS/MF

Lobel, Arnold.
*Frog and Toad Are
Friends.*
New York:
HarperTrophy, 1970.
An I Can Read book.
B-2

Lobel, Arnold.
Mouse Tales.
New York:
HarperTrophy Book,
1972.
An I Can Read book.
BR-2

Lobel, Arnold.
Owl at Home.
New York:

HarperTrophy, 1975.
An I Can Read book.
BR-2

Lobel, Arnold.
Small Pig.
New York:
HarperTrophy, 1969.
An I Can Read book.
BR-2

Lund, Jillian.
*Way Out West Lives a
Coyote Named Frank.*
New York: Dutton,
1993.
BR-2/MF

Maccarone, Grace.
Illus. by Betsy Lewin.
*Itchy, Itchy Chicken
Pox.*
New York: Scholastic,
1992. Hello Reader!
series, Level
1(preschool-Grade 1).
BR-1

Marshall, Edward.
Illus. by James Marshall.
Fox in Love.
New York: Puffin, 1982.
BR-2/MF

Marshall, Edward.
Illus. by James Marshall.
Fox on Wheels.
New York: Puffin, 1983.
BR-2/MF

Marshall, Edward.
Illus. by James Marshall.
Three by the Sea.
New York: Puffin, 1981.
BR-2

Marshall, James.
Fox Be Nimble.
New York: Puffin, 1990.
BR-2/MF

Marshall, James.
Fox on the Job.
New York: Puffin, 1988.
BR-2/MF

Marshall, James (retold by).
Goldilocks and the Three Bears.
New York: Scholastic, 1991.
BR-2/MF

McCully, Emily Arnold.
The Grandma Mix-Up.
New York:
HarperTrophy, 1988.
An I Can Read book.
BR-2/MF

Parish, Peggy.
Illus. by Wallace Tripp.
Play Ball, Amelia Bedelia.
New York:
HarperTrophy, 1972.
An I Can Read book.
BR-2/MF

Parker, Steve.
Human Body: Investigate and Understand Your Amazing Body.
New York: Dorling Kindersley, 1994.
AS/MF

Parry, Caroline.
Illus. by Michael Martchenk
Zoomerang a Boomerang: Poems to Make Your Belly Laugh.
New York: Puffin Books, 1993.
BR-2/MF

Paterson, Katherine.
Illus. by Jane Clark Brown.
The Smallest Cow in the World.
New York:
HarperTrophy, 1991.
An I Can Read book.
BR-2

Prelutsky, Jack.
Illus. by James Stevenson.
Something Big Has Been Here.
New York:
Greenwillow, 1990.
AS/MF

Prelutsky, Jack.
Illus. by James Stevenson.
The New Kid on the Block.
New York:
Greenwillow, 1984.
AS/MF

Prelutsky, Jack.
Illus. by Victoria Chess.
Rolling Harvey down the Hill.
New York: Mulberry, 1993.
MF

Prelutsky, Jack. (selector).
Illus. by Henrik Drescher.
Poems of A. Nonny Mouse.
New York: Dragonfly/ Alfred A. Knopf, 1989.
AS/MF

Rayner, Shoo.
My First Picture Joke Book.
New York: Picture Puffins, 1991.
MF

Rice, Eve.
Benny Bakes a Cake.
New York:
Greenwillow, 1993.
BR-1/BR-2

Rice, Eve (adapter).
Once in a Wood: Ten Tales from Aesop.
New York: Mulberry Books, 1993.
BR-2/MF

Robins, Joan.
Illus. by Sue Truesdall.
Addie Runs Away.
New York:
HarperTrophy, 1989.
An Early I Can Read book.
BR-2/MF

Rockwell, Anne and **Harlow Rockwell.**
Machines.
New York:
HarperTrophy, 1972.
E/BR-1

Rockwell, Harlow.
I Did It.
New York: Aladdin, 1974.
BR-2

Rockwell, Harlow.
Look at This.
New York: Aladdin, 1974.
BR-2

Rockwell, Harlow.
IDid It.
New York: Alladdin Books, 1974.
BR-2

Rockwell, Harlow.
Look at This.
New York: Aladdin, 1974.
BR-2

Rosenbloom, Joseph.
Illus. by Tim Raglin.
Deputy Dan Gets His Man.
New York: Random House, 1985.
MF

Royston, Angela.
Photography by Steve Shott.
Sea Animals.
New York: Aladdin, 1992.
AS/MF

Royston, Angela.
Photography by Steve Shott.
Ships and Boats.
New York: Aladdin. 1992.
AS/MF

Rylant, Cynthia.
Illus. by Sucie Stevenson.
Henry and Mudge: The First Book.
New York: Bradbury, 1987.
MF

Schwartz, Alvin.
Ten Copycats in a Boat and Other Riddles.
New York: HarperTrophy, 1980.
An I Can Read book.
BR-1/BR-2

Schwartz, Alvin.
Illus. by Syd Hoff.
I Saw You in the Bathtub and Other Folk Rhymes.
New York: HarperTrophy, 1989.
An I Can Read book.
BR-2

Schwartz, Alvin.
Illus. by Victoria Chess.
GHOSTS! Ghostly Tales from Folklore.
New York: Scholastic, 1991.
BR-2/MF

Schwartz, Alvin (reteller).
Illus. by Karen Ann Weinhaus.
There Is a Carrot in My Ear and Other Noodle Tales.
New York: HarperTrophy, 1982.
An I Can Read book.
BR-2

Sharmat, Marjorie Weinman.
Illus. by Jose Aruego and Ariane Dewey.
Mitchell is Moving.
New York: Aladdin, 1987.
MF

Sharmat, Marjorie Weinman.
Illus. by Marc Simot.
Nate the Great.
New York: Dell Young Yearling, 1972.
MF

Silverstein, Shel.
A Light in the Attic.
New York: Harper & Row, 1981.
AS/MF

Smith, Mavis.
A Snake Mistake.
New York: HarperCollins, 1991.
MF

Stadler, John.
Hooray for Snail!
New York: HarperTrophy, 1984.
BR-1/BR-2

Taylor, Barbara.
photographs by Frank Greenway.
Rain Forest: A Close-Up Look at the Natural World of a Rain Forest.
New York: Dorling Kindersley, 1992.
AS/MF

Thaler, Mike.
Illus. by Jared Lee.
A Hippopatomus Ate the Teacher.
New York: Avon, 1981.
MF/F

Udry, Janice May.
Illus. by Maurice Sendak.
Let's Be Enemies.
New York: HarperTrophy, 1961.
B-1

VanLeeuwen, Jean.
Illus. by Arnold Lobel.
Tales of Oliver Pig.
New York: Puffin, 1979.
B-2/MF

von Noorden, Djiann (editor).
The Lifesize Animal Counting Book.
New York: Dorling Kindersley, 1994.
AS/MF

Weiss, Nicki.
The First Night of Hannukkah.
New York: Grosset & Dunlap, 1992.
BR-2/MF

Wells, Rosemary.
Morris's Diappearing Bag: A Christmas Story.
New York: Puffin Pied Piper/Dial, 1975.
BR-2

Wells, Rosemary.
Noisy Nora.
New York: Scholastic, 1973.
BR-1

Wiseman, B.
Morris the Moose.
New York: HarperTrophy, 1989. An Early I Can Read book.
BR-1/BR-2

Ziefert, Harriet.
Illus. by Mavis Smith.
Let's Get A Pet.
New York: Viking, 1993.
AS/MF

Ziefert, Harriet.
Illus. by Richard Brown.
Nicky, 1-2-3.
New York: Puffin, 1995.
E/BR-1

Ziefert, Harriet.
Illus. Suzy Mandel.
Under the Water.
New York: Puffin, 1990.
BR-2/MF

Ziefert, James.
Illus. by Mavis Smith.
Harry Goes To Day Camp.
New York: Puffin, 1990.
BR-1/BR-2

Zion, Gene.
Illus. by Margaret Bloy Graham.
Harry and the Lady Next Door.
New York: HarperTrophy, 1960.
An Early I Can Read book.
BR-2

By Title

Addie Runs Away.
Robins, Joan.
Illus. by Sue Truesdall.
New York:
HarperTrophy, 1989.
An Early I Can Read
book.
BR-2/MF

Arthur's Pet Business.
Brown, Marc.
Boston: Little, Brown
and Company, 1990.
MF/F

**Aunt Eater Loves a
Mystery.**
Cushman, Doug.
New York:
HarperTrophy 1987.
An I Can Read book.
BR-2

**Belly Laughs: Food Jokes
and Riddles.**
Keller, Charles.
illlus. by Ron Fritz.
New York: Simon &
Schuster, 1990.
MF/F

Benny Bakes a Cake.
Rice, Eve.
New York:
Greenwillow, 1993.
BR-1/BR-2

**The Berenstain Bears
and the Big Road Race.**
Berenstain, Stan and Jan
Berenstain.
New York: Random
House, 1987.
BR-1

**The Best Teacher in the
World.**
Chardiet, Bernice and
Grace Maccarone.
Illus. by G. Brian Karas.
New York: Scholastic,
1990.
MF

Bing Bang Boing.
Florian, Douglas.
New York: Harcourt
Brace & Company, 1994.
AS/MF

Building a House.
Barton, Bryon.
New York: Mulberry,
1981.
BR-2

Buggy Riddles.
Hall, Katy and Lisa
Eisenberg.
Illus. by Simms Taback.
New York: Puffin, 1986.
Puffin Easy-to-Read.
MF

Calf.
Ling, Mary.
photographed by Gordon
Clayton.
New York: Dorling
Kindersley, 1993.
AS/MF

The Carrot Seed.
Krauss, Ruth. Illus. by
Crockett Johnson.
New York: Harper and
Row, 1945.
BR-2

A Chef.
Florian, Douglas.
New York:
Greenwillow, 1992.
AS/MF

Chicago and the Cat.
Koontz, Robin Michal.
New York: Cobblehill
Books, 1993.
MF

City Street.
Florian, Douglas.
New York:
Greenwillow, 1990.
AS/MF

Danny and the Dinosaur.
Hoff, Syd.
New York: Scholastic,
1958.
BR-2

A Dark Dark Tale.
Brown, Ruth.
New York: Puffin Pied
Piper, 1984.
E/BR-1

**Deputy Dan Gets His
Man.**
Rosenbloom, Joseph.
Illus. by Tim Raglin.
New York: Random
House, 1985.
MF

Dinosaur Day.
Donnelly, Liza.
New York: Scholastic,
1987.
BR-1

Dinosaur Garden.
Donnelly, Liza.

New York: Scholastic,
1990.
E/BR-1

Dog.
Clutton-Brock, Juliet.
New York: Alfred A.
Knopf, 1991.
AS/MF

**The Dog That Pitched a
No-Hitter.**
Christopher, Matt.
Boston: Little, Brown
and Company, 1988.
MF/F

**Easy as Pie: A Guessing
Game of Saying.**
Folsom, Marcia and
Michael Folsom.
Illus. by Jack Kent.
New York: Clarion,
1985.
AS/MF

Eddie and Teddy.
Clarke, Gus.
New York: Mulberry
Books, 1990.
BR-2

The Egg.
Jeunesse, Gallimard and
Pascale de Bourgoing.
Illus. by Rene Mettler.
New York: Scholastic,
1989.
AS/MF

**The First Night of
Hannukkah.**
Weiss, Nicki.
New York: Grosset &
Dunlap, 1992.
BR-2/MF

Fishing.
Engel, Diana.
New York: Macmillan,
1993.
MF/F

The Flat Man.
Impey, Rose.
Illus. by Moira Kemp.
New York: Dell Young
Yearling, 1988.
MF

Fox Be Nimble.
Marshall, James.
New York: Puffin, 1990.
BR-2/MF

Fox in Love.
Marshall, Edward.
Illus. by James Marshall.
New York: Puffin, 1982.
BR-2/MF

Fox on the Job.
Marshall, James.
New York: Puffin, 1988.
BR-2/MF

Fox on Wheels.
Marshall, Edward.
Illus. by James Marshall.
New York: Puffin, 1983.
BR-2/MF

**Frog and Toad Are
Friends.**
Lobel, Arnold.
New York:
HarperTrophy, 1970.
An I Can Read book.
B-2

**GHOSTS! Ghostly Tales
from Folklore.**
Schwartz, Alvin.
Illus. by Victoria Chess.
New York: Scholastic,
1991.
BR-2/MF

Gino Badino.
Engel, Diana.
New York: Morrow
Junior Books, 1991.
MF/F

**Goldilocks and the Three
Bears.**
Marshall, James (retold
by).
New York: Scholastic,
1991.
BR-2/MF

The Grandma Mix-Up.
McCully, Emily Arnold.
New York:
HarperTrophy, 1988.
An I Can Read book.
BR-2/MF

Grizzy Riddles.
Hall, Katy and Lisa
Eisenberg. Illus. by
Nicole Rubel.
New York: Puffin, 1989.
Puffin Easy to Read.
MF

Growing Vegetable Soup.
Ehlert, Lois.
New York: Scholastic,
1987.
E/BR-1

**Henry and Mudge: The
First Book.**
Rylant, Cynthia.
Illus. by Sucie
Stevenson.
New York: Bradbury,
1987.
MF

Harry and the Lady Next Door.
Zion, Gene.
Illus. by Margaret Bloy
Graham.
New York:
HarperTrophy, 1960.
An Early I Can Read
book.
BR-2

Harry Goes to Day Camp.
Ziefert, James.
Illus. by Mavis Smith.
New York: Puffin, 1990.
BR-1/BR-2

Here Comes the Strikeout.
Kessler, Leonard.
New York:
HarperTrophy, 1965. An
I Can Read book.
BR-2

A Hippopotomus Ate the Teacher.
Thaler, Mike.
Illus. by Jared Lee.
New York: Avon, 1981.
MF/F

Hooray for Snail!
Stadler, John.
New York:
HarperTrophy, 1984.
BR-1/BR-2

The Horse in Harry's Room.
Hoff, Syd.
New York:
HarperTrophy, 1970. An
Early I Can Read book.
BR-1/BR-2

Human Body: Investigate and Understand Your Amazing Body.
Parker, Steve.
New York: Dorling
Kindersley,1994.
AS/MF

I Did It.
Rockwell, Harlow.
New York: Aladdin,
1974.
BR-2

I Like Me!
Carlson, Nancy.
New York: Puffin Books,
1988
E/B-1

I Saw You in the Bathtub and Other Folk Rhymes.
Schwartz, Alvin.
Illus. by Syd Hoff.
New York:
HarperTrophy, 1989.
An I Can Read book.
BR-2

Itchy, Itchy Chicken Pox.
Maccarone, Grace.
Illus. by Betsy Lewin.
New York: Scholastic,
1992. Hello Reader!
series, Level 1
(preschool-Grade 1).
BR-1

Jim Meets the Thing.
Cohen, Miriam.
Illus. by Lillian Hoban.
New York: Dell Young
Yearling, 1981.
BR-2

Kick, Pass, and Run.
Kessler, Leonard.
New York:
HarperTrophy, 1966. An
I Can Read book.
BR-2

Kit and Kat.
dePaola, Tomie.
New York: Grosset and
Dunlap, 1994.
All Aboard Reading,
Level 1.
E/BR-1

Knock! Knock!
Hawkins, Colin and
Jacqui Hawkins.
New York: Aladdin,
1991.
BR-2/MF

Leo and Emily.
Brandenberg, Franz.
Illus. by Aliki.
New York: Dell Young
Yearling, 1981.
BR-2/MF

Leo, Zack, and Emmie.
Ehrlich, Amy.
Illus. by Steven Kellog.
New York: Dial Books
for Young Readers, 1981.
BR-2/MF

Let's Be Enemies.
Udry, Janice May.
Illus. by Maurice
Sendak.
New York:
HarperTrophy, 1961.
B-1

Let's Get A Pet.
Ziefert, Harriet.
Illus. by Mavis Smith.
New York: Viking, 1993.
AS/MF

Liar, Liar, Pants on Fire!
Cohen, Miriam.
Illus. by Lillian Hoban.
New York: Dell Young
Yearling, 1985.
BR-2

**The Lifesize Animal
Counting Book.**
von Noorden, Djiann
(editor).
New York: Dorling
Kindersley, 1994.
AS/MF

A Light in the Attic.
Silverstein, Shel.
New York:
HarperCollins, 1981.
AS/MF

The Little Red Hen.
Galdone, Paul.
New York: Clarion,
1973.
BR-1/BR-2

Look at This.
Rockwell, Harlow.
New York: Aladdin,
1974.
BR-2

Machines.
Rockwell, Anne and
Harlow Rockwell.
New York:
HarperTrophy, 1972.
E/BR-1

Mine's the Best.
Bonsall, Crosby.
New York:
HarperTrophy, 1973. An
Early I Can Read book.
BR-1

The Missing Tooth.
Cole, Joanna.
Illus. by Marilyn Hafner.
New York: Random

House, 1988.
BR-2/MF

Mitchell is Moving.
Sharmat, Marjorie
Weinman.
Illus. by Jose Aruego and
Ariane Dewey.
New York: Aladdin,
1987.
MF

Monkeys and Apes.
Barrett, N.S.
New York: Franklin
Watts, 1988.
AS/MF

More Spaghetti, I Say!
Gelman, Rita Golden.
Illus. by Jack Kent.
New York: Scholastic,
1977.
BR-1/BR-2

Morris the Moose.
Wiseman, B.
New York:
HarperTrophy, 1989. (An
Early I Can Read Book).
BR-1/BR-2

**Morris's Diappearing
Bag: A Christmas Story.**
Wells, Rosemary.
New York: Puffin Pied
Piper/Dial, 1975.
BR-2

Mouse Tales.
Lobel, Arnold.
New York:
HarperTrophy Book,
1972.
An I Can Read book.
BR-2

Mrs. Brice's Mice.
Hoff, Syd.
New York:
HarperTrophy, 1988.

An Early I Can Read
Book
BR-1/BR-2

**Munching Poems About
Eating.**
Hopkins, Lee Bennett
(selector).
Boston: Little, Brown,
1985.
AS/MF

My First Number Book.
Heinst, Marie.
New York: Dorling
Kindersley, 1992.
AS/MF

**My First Picture Joke
Book.**
Rayner, Shoo.
New York: Picture
Puffins, 1991.
MF

Nate the Great.
Sharmat, Marjorie
Weinman. Illus. by Marc
Simot.
New York: Dell Young
Yearling, 1972.
MF

**The New Kid on the
Block.**
Prelutsky, Jack.
Illus. by James
Stevenson.
New York:
Greenwillow, 1984.
AS/MF

A Nickel Buys a Rhyme.
Benjamin, Alan. Illus. by
Karen Lee Schmidt.
New York: Morrow
Junior, 1993.
AS/MF

Nicky, 1-2-3.
Ziefert, Harriet.
Illus. by Richard Brown.
New York: Puffin, 1995.
E/BR-1

Noisy Nora.
Wells, Rosemary.
New York: Scholastic,
1973.
BR-1

Old Turtle's Baseball Stories.
Kessler, Leonard.
New York: Dell Young
Yearling, 1982.
BR-2

Old Turtle's 90 Knock-Knocks, Jokes, and Riddles.
Kessler, Leonard.
New York: Mulberry,
1991.
BR-2/MF

Once in a Wood: Ten Tales from Aesop.
Rice, Eve (adapter).
New York: Mulberry
Books, 1993.
BR-2/MF

Owl at Home.
Lobel, Arnold.
New York:
HarperTrophy, 1975.
An I Can Read book.
BR-2

Penrod Again.
Christian, Mary Blount.
Illus. by Jane Dyer.
New York: Aladdin
Books, 1990.
BR-2

Pickle Things.
Brown, Marc.
New York: Parents
Magazine Press/Putnam
& Grosset Book Group,
1980.
BR-1/BR-2

Play Ball, Amelia Bedelia.
Parish, Peggy.
Illus. by Wallace Tripp.
New York:
HarperTrophy, 1972.
An I Can Read book.
BR-2/MF

Poems of A. Nonny Mouse.
Prelutsky, Jack
(selector).
Illus. by Henrik
Drescher.
New York: Dragonfly/
Alfred A. Knopf, 1989.
AS/MF

Rain Forest: A Close-Up Look at the Natural World of a Rain Forest.
Taylor, Barbara.
Photographs by Frank
Greenway.
New York: Dorling
Kindersley, 1992.
AS/MF

Reptiles.
Brennan, Frank. Illus. by
Malcolm Livingstone.
New York: Aladdin,
1992.
AS/MF

Roller Skates!
Calmenson, Stephanie.
Illus. by True Kelley
New York: Scholastic,
1992.
Hello Reader! series,
Level 2 (K-Grade 2).
BR-1/BR-2

Rolling Harvey down the Hill.
Prelutsky, Jack.
Illus. by Victoria Chess.
New York: Mulberry,
1993.
MF

Sea Animals.
Royston, Angela.
Photography by Steve
Shott.
New York: Aladdin,
1992.
AS/MF

Sharks in Action
Gay, Tanner Ottley.
Illus. by Jean Cassels.
New York: Aladdin,
1990.
AS/MF

Ships and Boats.
Royston, Angela.
Photography by Steve
Shott.
New York: Aladdin,
1992.
AS/MF

The Silliest Joke Book Ever.
Hartman, Victoria.
Illus. by R.W. Alleyn
New York: Lothrop, Lee
& Shepard Books, 1993.
AS/MF

Simpson Snail Sings.
Himmelman, John.
New York: Dutton,
1992.
MF

Six Sick Sheep: 101 Tongue Twisters.
Cole, Joanna and
Stephanie Calmenson.
Illus. by Alan Tiegreen.

New York: Beech Tree, 1993.
MF

Small Pig.
Lobel, Arnold.
New York: HarperTrophy, 1969.
An I Can Read book.
BR-2

The Smallest Cow in the World.
Paterson, Katherine.
Illus. by Jane Clark Brown.
New York: HarperTrophy, 1991.
An I Can Read book.
BR-2

A Snake Mistake.
Smith, Mavis.
New York: HarperCollins, 1991.
MF

Something Big Has Been Here.
Prelutsky, Jack.
Illus. by James Stevenson.
New York: Greenwillow, 1990.
AS/MF

Spot Goes to School.
Hill, Eric.
New York: Puffin, 1984.
E

Stop Thief!
Kalan, Robert.
Illus. by Yossi Abolafia.
New York: Greenwillow, 1993.
BR-2

Tales of Oliver Pig.
VanLeeuwen, Jean.
Illus. by Arnold Lobel.

New York: Puffin, 1979.
B-2/MF

The Teeny-Tiny Woman: A Ghost Story.
Galdone, Paul.
New York: Clarion, 1984.
E/BR-1

Ten Apples Up on Top.
LeSeig, Theo.
Illus. by Roy McKie.
New York: Random House Beginner Books, 1961. (Out of print?)
E/BR-1

Ten Copycats in a Boat and Other Riddles.
Schwartz, Alvin.
New York: HarperTrophy, 1980.
An I Can Read book.
BR-1/BR-2

There Is a Carrot in My Ear and Other Noodle Tales.
Schwartz, Alvin (reteller). Illus. by Karen Ann Weinhaus.
New York: HarperTrophy, 1982.
An I Can Read book.
BR-2

Three Aesop Fox Fables.
New York: Clarion, 1971.
MF

Three by the Sea.
Marshall, Edward.
Illus. by James Marshall.
New York: Puffin, 1981.
BR-2

Three Happy Birthdays.
Caseley, Judith.
New York: Mulberry

Books,1989.
BR-2

The Three Little Pigs.
Galdone, Paul.
New York: Clarion, 1970.
BR-1/BR-2

Tongue Twisters.
Keller, Charles.
Illus. by Ron Fritz.
New York: Simon & Schuster, 1989.
AS/MF

The Trouble with Uncle.
Cole, Babette.
Boston: Little, Brown and Company, 1992.
MF

Under the Water.
Ziefert, Harriet.
Illus. by Suzy Mandel.
New York: Puffin, 1990.
BR-2/MF

Way Out West Lives a Coyote Named Frank.
Lund, Jillian.
New York: Dutton, 1993.
BR-2/MF

When This Box Is Full.
Lillie, Patricia.
Illus. by Donald Crews.
New York: Greenwillow, 1993.
BR-1/BR-2

What a Pest!
Cocca-Leffler, Maryann.
New York: Grosset & Dunlap, 1994.
All Aboard Reading.
Level 1.
E/BR-1

What's On the Menu?
Goldstein, Bobbye S.
(selector).
Illus. by Chris L.
Demarest.
New York: Viking, 1992.
AS/MF

***The Witch Goes to
School.***
Bridwell, Norman.
New York: Scholastic,
1992.
Hello Reader! series,
Level 3 (Grade 1 and 2).
BR-2

***Your Dog Might Be a
Werewolf, Your Toes
Could All Explode.***
Greenberg, David.
Illus. by George Ulrich.
New York: Bantam First
Skylark, 1992.
MF/F

***Yours Till Banana Splits:
201 Autograph Rhymes.***
Cole, Joanna and
Stephanie Calmenson.
Illus. by Alan Tiegreen.
New York: Beech Tree,
1995.
MF

***Zoomerang a
Boomerang: Poems to
Make Your Belly Laugh.***
Parry, Caroline.
Illus. by Michael
Martchenk
New York: Puffin Books,
1993.
BR-2/MF

By Level

E

Hill, Eric.
Spot Goes to School.
New York: Puffin, 1984.

E/R-1

Carlson, Nancy.
I Like Me!
New York: Puffin Books,
1988

Brown, Ruth.
A Dark Dark Tale.
New York: Puffin Pied
Piper, 1984.

Cocca-Leffler, Maryann.
What a Pest!
New York: Grosset &
Dunlap, 1994.
All Aboard Reading.
Level 1.

dePaola, Tomie.
Kit and Kat.
New York: Grosset and
Dunlap, 1994.
All Aboard Reading,
Level 1.

Donnelly, Liza.
Dinosaur Garden.
New York: Scholastic,
1990.

Ehlert, Lois.
*Growing Vegetable
Soup.*
New York: Scholastic,
1987.

Galdone, Paul.
*The Teeny-Tiny Woman:
A Ghost Story.*
New York: Clarion,
1984.

LeSeig, Theo.
Illus. by Roy McKie.
Ten Apples Up on Top.
New York: Random
House Beginner Books,
1961. (Out of print?)

Ziefert, Harriet.
Illus. by Richard Brown.
Nicky, 1-2-3.
New York: Puffin, 1995.

**Rockwell, Anne and
Harlow Rockwell.**
Machines.
New York:
HarperTrophy, 1972.

BR-1

**Berenstain, Stan and Jan
Berenstain.**
*The Berenstain Bears
and the Big Road Race.*
New York: Random
House, 1987.

Bonsall, Crosby.
Mine's the Best.
New York:
HarperTrophy (An Early
I Can Read Book), 1973.

Donnelly, Liza.
Dinosaur Day.
New York: Scholastic,
1987.

Maccarone, Grace.
Illus. by Betsy Lewin.
*Itchy, Itchy Chicken
Pox.*
New York: Scholastic,

1992. Hello Reader!
series, Level
1(preschool-Grade 1).

Udry, Janice May.
Illus. by Maurice
Sendak.
Let's Be Enemies.
New York:
HarperTrophy, 1961.

Wells, Rosemary.
Noisy Nora.
New York: Scholastic,
1973.

BR-1/BR-2

Brown, Marc.
Pickle Things.
New York: Parents
Magazine Press/Putnam
& Grosset Book Group,
1980.

Calmenson, Stephanie.
Illus. by True Kelley
Roller Skates!
New York: Scholastic,
1992.
Hello Reader! series,
Level 2 (K-Grade 2).

Galdone, Paul.
The Little Red Hen.
New York: Clarion,
1973.

Galdone, Paul.
The Three Little Pigs.
New York: Clarion,
1970.

Gelman, Rita Golden.
Illus. by Jack Kent.
More Spaghetti, I Say!

New York: Scholastic, 1977.

Hoff, Syd.
Mrs. Brice's Mice.
New York: HarperTrophy, 1988. An Early I Can Read book.

Hoff, Syd.
The Horse in Harry's Room.
New York: HarperTrophy, 1970. An Early I Can Read book.

Lillie, Patricia.
Illus. by Donald Crews. *When This Box Is Full.*
New York: Greenwillow, 1993.

Nagel, Karen Berman.
Illus. Brian Schatell. *Two Crazy Pigs.*
New York: Scholastic, 1992. Hello Reader! series, Level 2 (K–Grade 2).

Rice, Eve.
Benny Bakes a Cake.
New York: Greenwillow, 1993.

Stadler, John.
Hooray for Snail!
New York: HarperTrophy,1984.

Wiseman, B.
Morris the Moose.
New York: HarperTrophy, 1989. An Early I Can Read book.

Ziefert, James.
Illus. by Mavis Smith. *Harry Goes To Day Camp.*
New York: Puffin, 1990.

122

Schwartz, Alvin.
Ten Copycats in a Boat and Other Riddles.
New York: HarperTrophy, 1980. An I Can Read book.

BR-2

Barton, Bryon.
Building a House.
New York: Mulberry, 1981.

Bridwell, Norman.
The Witch Goes to School.
New York: Scholastic, 1992.
Hello Reader! series, Level 3 (Grade 1 and 2).

Caseley, Judith.
Three Happy Birthdays.
New York: Mulberry Books,1989.

Christian, Mary Blount.
Illus. by Jane Dyer. *Penrod Again.*
New York: Aladdin Books, 1990.

Clarke, Gus.
Eddie and Teddy.
New York: Mulberry Books, 1990.

Cohen, Miriam.
Illus. by Lillian Hoban. *Jim Meets the Thing.*
New York: Dell Young Yearling, 1981.

Cohen, Miriam.
Illus. by Lillian Hoban. *Liar, Liar, Pants on Fire!*
New York: Dell Young Yearling, 1985.

Cushman, Doug.
Aunt Eater Loves a

Mystery.
New York: HarperTrophy, 1987. An I Can Read book.

Hoff, Syd.
Danny and the Dinosaur.
New York: Scholastic, 1958.

Kalan, Robert.
Illus. by Yossi Abolafia. *Stop Thief!*
New York: Greenwillow, 1993.

Kessler, Leonard.
Here Comes the Strikeout.
New York: HarperTrophy, 1965. An I Can Read book..

Kessler, Leonard.
Kick, Pass, and Run.
New York: HarperTrophy, 1966.

Kessler, Leonard.
Old Turtle's Baseball Stories.
New York: Dell Young Yearling, 1982.

Krauss, Ruth.
Illus. by Crockett Johnson. *The Carrot Seed.*
New York: Harper and Row, 1945.

Lobel, Arnold.
Frog and Toad Are Friends.
New York: HarperTrophy, 1970. An I Can Read book.

Lobel, Arnold.
Mouse Tales.
New York:

HarperTrophy Book, 1972. An I Can Read book.

Lobel, Arnold.
Owl at Home.
New York: HarperTrophy, 1975. An I Can Read book.

Lobel, Arnold.
Small Pig.
New York: HarperTrophy, 1969. An I Can Read book.

Marshall, Edward.
Illus. by James Marshall.
Three by the Sea.
New York: Puffin, 1981.

McCully, Emily Arnold.
The Grandma Mix-Up.
New York: HarperTrophy, 1988. An I Can Read book.

Parish, Peggy.
Illus. by Leonard Kessler.
Be Ready at Eight.
New York: Aladdin Books, 1979.

Paterson, Katherine.
Illus. by Jane Clark Brown.
The Smallest Cow in the World.
New York: HarperTrophy, 1991. An I Can Read book.

Rockwell, Harlow.
I Did It.
New York: Aladdin, 1974.

Rockwell, Harlow.
Look at This.
New York: Aladdin, 1974.

Schwartz, Alvin.
Illus. by Syd Hoff.
I Saw You in the Bathtub and Other Folk Rhymes.
New York: HarperTrophy, 1989. An I Can Read book.

Schwartz, Alvin (reteller).
Illus. by Karen Ann Weinhaus.
There Is a Carrot in my Ear and Other Noodle Tales.
New York: HarperTrophy, 1982. An I Can Read book.

Wells, Rosemary.
Morris's Diappearing Bag: A Christmas Story.
New York: Puffin Pied Piper/Dial, 1975.

Zion, Gene.
Illus. by Margaret Bloy Graham.
Harry and the Lady Next Door.
New York: HarperTrophy, 1960. An Early I Can Read book.

BR-2/MF

Brandenberg, Franz.
Illus. by Aliki.
Leo and Emily.
New York: Dell Young Yearling, 1981.

Cole, Joanna.
Illus. by Marilyn Hafner.
The Missing Tooth.
New York: Random House, 1988.

Ehrlich, Amy.
Illus. by Steven Kellog.
Leo, Zack, and Emmie.
New York: Dial Books for Young Readers, 1981.

Hawkins, Colin and **Jacqui Hawkins.**
Knock! Knock!
New York: Aladdin, 1991.

Kessler, Leonard.
Old Turtle's 90 Knock-Knocks, Jokes, and Riddles.
New York: Mulberry, 1991.

Lund, Jillian.
Way Out West Lives a Coyote Named Frank.
New York: Dutton, 1993.

Marshall, Edward.
Illus. by James Marshall.
Fox in Love.
New York: Puffin, 1982.

Marshall, Edward.
Illus. by James Marshall.
Fox on Wheels.
New York: Puffin, 1983.

Marshall, James.
Fox Be Nimble.
New York: Puffin, 1990.

Marshall, James.
Fox on the Job.
New York: Puffin, 1988.

Marshall, James (retold by).
Goldilocks and the Three Bears.
New York: Scholastic, 1991.

O'Connor, Jane.
Illus. by Brian Karas.

Eek! Stories to Make You Shriek. New York: Grosset & Dunlap, 1992. All Aboard Reading, Level 2 (Grades 1-3).

Parish, Peggy.
Illus. by Wallace Tripp. *Come Back, Amelia Bedelia.* New York: HarperTrophy, 1971. An I Can Read book.

Parish, Peggy.
Illus. by Wallace Tripp. *Play Ball, Amelia Bedelia.* New York: HarperTrophy, 1972. An I Can Read book.

Parry, Caroline.
Illus. by Michael Martchenk *Zoomerang a Boomerang: Poems to Make Your Belly Laugh.* New York: Puffin Books, 1993.

Rice, Eve (adapter).
Once in a Wood: Ten Tales from Aesop. New York: Mulberry Books, 1993.

Robins, Joan.
Illus. by Sue Truesdall. *Addie Runs Away.* New York: HarperTrophy, 1989. An Early I Can Read book.

Schwartz, Alvin.
Illus. by Victoria Chess. *GHOSTS! Ghostly Tales from Folklore.*

New York: Scholastic, 1991.

Weiss, Nicki.
The First Night of Hannukkah. New York: Grosset & Dunlap, 1992.

VanLeeuwen, Jean.
Illus. by Arnold Lobel. *Tales of Oliver Pig.* New York: Puffin, 1979.

Ziefert, Harriet.
Illus. Suzy Mandel. *Under the Water.* New York: Puffin, 1990.

MF

Chardiet, Bernice and **Grace Maccarone.**
Illus. by G. Brian Karas. *The Best Teacher in the World.* New York: Scholastic, 1990.

Cole, Babette.
The Trouble with Uncle. Boston: Little, Brown and Company, 1992.

Cole, Joanna and **Stephanie Calmenson.**
Illus. by Alan Tiegreen. *Six Sick Sheep: 101 Tongue Twisters.* New York: Beech Tree, 1993.

Cole, Joanna and **Stephanie Calmenson.**
Illus. by Alan Tiegreen. *Yours Till Banana Splits: 201 Autograph Rhymes.* New York: Beech Tree, 1995.

Galdone, Paul.
Three Aesop Fox Fables. New York: Clarion, 1971.

Hall, Katy and **Lisa Eisenberg.**
Illus. by Simms Taback. *Buggy Riddles.* New York: Puffin, 1986. Easy-to-Read.

Hall, Katy and **Lisa Eisenberg.**
Illus. by Nicole Rubel. *Grizzly Riddles.* New York: Puffin, 1989. Puffin Easy-to-Read.

Himmelman, John.
Simpson Snail Sings. New York: Dutton, 1992.

Impey, Rose.
Illus. by Moira Kemp. *The Flat Man.* New York: Dell Young Yearling, 1988.

Koontz, Robin Michal.
Chicago and the Cat. New York: Cobblehill Books, 1993.

Prelutsky, Jack.
Illus. by Victoria Chess. *Rolling Harvey down the Hill.* New York: Mulberry, 1993.

Rayner, Shoo.
My First Picture Joke Book. New York: Picture Puffins, 1991.

Rosenbloom, Joseph.
Illus. by Tim Raglin. *Deputy Dan Gets His Man.*

New York: Random House, 1985.

Rylant, Cynthia.
Illus. by Sucie Stevenson.
Henry and Mudge: The First Book.
New York: Bradbury, 1987.

Sharmat, Marjorie Weinman.
Illus. by Jose Aruego and Ariane Dewey.
Mitchell is Moving.
New York: Aladdin, 1987.

Sharmat, Marjorie Weinman.
Illus. by Marc Simot.
Nate the Great.
New York: Dell Young Yearling, 1972.

Smith, Mavis.
A Snake Mistake.
New York: HarperCollins, 1991.

MF/F

Brown, Marc.
Arthur's Pet Business.
Boston: Little, Brown and Company, 1990

Christopher, Matt.
The Dog That Pitched a No-Hitter.
Boston: Little, Brown and Company, 1988.

Engel, Diana.
Fishing.
New York: Macmillan, 1993.

Engel, Diana.
Gino Badino.

New York: Morrow Junior Books, 1991.

Greenberg, David.
Illus. by George Ulrich.
Your Dog Might Be a Werewolf, Your Toes Could All Explode.
New York: Bantam First Skylark, 1992.

Thaler, Mike.
Illus. by Jared Lee.
A Hippopotomus Ate the Teacher.
New York: Avon, 1981.

Keller, Charles.
illlus. by Ron Fritz.
Belly Laughs: Food Jokes and Riddles.
New York: Simon & Schuster, 1990.

AS/MF

Barrett, N.S.
Monkeys and Apes.
New York: Franklin Watts, 1988.

Brennan, Frank.
Illus. by Malcolm Livingstone.
Reptiles.
New York: Aladdin, 1992.

Clutton-Brock, Juliet.
Dog.
New York: Alfred A. Knopf, 1991.

Florian, Douglas.
A Chef.
New York: Greenwillow, 1992.

Florian, Douglas.
City Street.
New York: Greenwillow, 1990.

Gay, Tanner Ottley.
Illus. by Jean Cassels.
Sharks in Action
New York: Aladdin, 1990.

Heinst, Marie.
My First Number Book.
New York: Dorling Kindersley, 1992.

Jeunesse, Gallimard and **Pascale de Bourgoing.**
Illus. by Rene Mettler.
The Egg.
New York: Scholastic, 1989.

Ling, Mary.
photographed by Gordon Clayton.
Calf.
New York: Dorling Kindersley, 1993.

Micklethwait, Lucy (selector).
I Spy Two Eyes: Number in Art.
New York: Greenwillow, 1993.

Parker, Steve.
Human Body: Investigate and Understand Your Amazing Body.
New York: Dorling Kindersley, 1994.

Royston, Angela.
Photography by Steve Shott.
Sea Animals.
New York: Aladdin, 1992.

Royston, Angela.
Photography by Steve Shott.
Ships and Boats.

New York: Aladdin, 1992.

Taylor, Barbara.
photographs by Frank Greenway.
Rain Forest: A Close-Up Look at the Natural World of a Rain Forest.
New York: Dorling Kindersley, 1992.

von Noorden, Djiann (editor).
The Lifesize Animal Counting Book.
New York: Dorling Kindersley, 1994.

Ziefert, Harriet.
Illus. by Mavis Smith.
Let's Get A Pet.
New York: Viking, 1993.

Folsom, Marcia and **Michael Folsom.**
Illus. by Jack Kent.
Easy as Pie : A Guessing Game of Saying.
New York: Clarion, 1985.

Hartman, Victoria.
Illus. by R.W. Alley.n
The Silliest Joke Book Ever.
New York: Lothrop, Lee & Shepard Books, 1993.

Keller, Charles.
Illus. by Ron Fritz.
Tongue Twisters.
New York: Simon & Schuster, 1989.

Florian, Douglas.
Bing Bang Boing.
New York: Harcourt Brace & Company, 1994.

Goldstein, Bobbye S.
(selector).

Illus. by Chris L. Demarest.
What's On the Menu?
New York: Viking, 1992.

Hopkins, Lee Bennett
(selector).
Munching Poems About Eating.
Boston: Little, Brown, 1985.

Prelutsky, Jack.
Illus. by James Stevenson.
Something Big Has Been Here.
New York: Greenwillow, 1990.

Prelutsky, Jack.
Illus. by James Stevenson.
The New Kid on the Block.
New York: Greenwillow, 1984.

Silverstein, Shel.
A Light in the Attic.
New York: Harper & Row, 1981.

Prelutsky, Jack (selector).
Illus. by Henrik Drescher.
Poems of A. Nonny Mouse.
New York: Dragonfly/ Alfred A. Knopf, 1989.

Benjamin, Alan.
Illus. by Karen Lee Schmidt.
A Nickel Buys a Rhyme.
New York: Morrow Junior, 1993.

Bibliography

Barrs, Myra, Ellis, Sue, Hester, Hilary, and Thomas, Anne. (1988). *The Primary Language Record: Handbook for Teachers*. Portsmouth, NH: Heinemann.

Bissex, Glenda L. (1980) *GNYS AT WRK: A Child Learns to Write and Read*. Cambridge, MA: Harvard University Press.

Botel, Morton, and Seaver, JoAnn Tuttle. (1987). *Literacy Network Handbook: Reading, Writing, and Oral Communication Across the Curriculum*. Levittown, PA: Morton Botel/JoAnn Seaver.

Cambourne, Brian. (1988). *The Whole Story: Natural Learning and the Acquisition of Literacy in the Classroom*. Richmond Hill, Ontario, Canada: Scholastic TAB Publications Ltd.

Carini, Particia. (1988). "Another Way of Looking." In K. Jerris and A. Tobler, eds. *Education for Democracy*. Weston, MA: The Cambridge School.

Clay, Marie M. (December 1991). "Introducing a New Storybook to Young Readers." *The Reading Teacher, 45,* 264–273.

Cochran-Smith, Marilyn. (1984). *The Making of a Reader*. Norwood, NJ: Ablex.

Fielding, Linda, and Roller, Cathy. (May 1992). "Making Difficult Books Accessible and Easy Books Acceptable." *The Reading Teacher, 45,* 678–685.

Fox, Mem. (1993). *Radical Reflections: Passionate Opinions on Teaching, Learning, and Living*. NY: Harcourt Brace & Company.

Gallas, Karen. (February 1991). "Art as Episternology: Enabling Children to Know What They Know." *Harvard Educational Review, 61,* 40–50.

Goodman, Kenneth. (1986). *What's Whole in Whole Language?* Portsmouth, NH: Heinemann. Ontario, Canada: Scholastic.

Graves, Donald H. (1990). *Discover Your Own Literacy*. Portsmouth, NH: Heinemann.

Graves, Michael F. and Graves, Bonnie B. (1994). *Scaffolding Reading Experiences*. Norwood, MA: Christoper-Gordon.

Heath, Shirley Brice. (1983). *Ways With Words: Language, Life and Work in Communities and Classroom*. London: Cambridge University Press.

Holdaway, Don. (1979). *The Foundations of Literacy*. New York: Ashton Scholastic.

Hoyt, Linda. (April 1992). "Many Ways of Knowing: Using Drama, Oral Interactions, and the Visual Arts to Enhance Reading Comprehension." *The Reading Teacher, 45,* 580–584.

Huck, Charlotte S. (November 1992). "Literacy and Literature." *Language Arts, 69,* 520–526.

Johnston, Peter. (1992). *Constructive Evaluation of Literate Activity*. NY: Longman.

Lewis, C.S. (1978). "On Stories." In

Margaret Meck, Aidan Warlow, and Griselda Barton (eds.), *The Cool Web: The Pattern of Children's Reading.* (pp. 76-90). NY: Atheneum.

Lynch, Priscilla. (1986). *Using Big Books and Predictable Books.* NY: Scholastic.

Mahy, Margaret. (April 1993). "Reading and READING: The Story and the Speech Given at the Annual Convention of Skill." The International Reading Association, San Antonio.

Martinez, Miriam, and Nash, Marcia F. (March 1991). "Bookalogues: Talking About Children's Books; Literature in a Chapter 1 Program." *Language Arts, 68,* 241–247.

Martinez, Miriam, and Nash, Marcia F. (September 1991). "Bookalogues: Talking About Children's Books: Books for Good Beginnings." *Language Arts, 68,* 410–416.

McGill-Franzen, Anne. (February 1993). "I Could Read the Words!: Selecting Good Books for Inexperienced Readers." *The Reading Teacher, 46,* 424–426.

Ninio, Anat and Bruner, Jerome (1978). "The Achievement and Antecedents of Labelling." *Journal of Child Language, 5,* 1–15.

Nolan, Elizabeth A., and Berry, Martha. (April 1993). "Learning to Listen." *The Reading Teacher, 46,* 606–608.

Peterson, Barbara. (1991). "Selecting Books for Beginning Readers." In D. DeFord, C. Lyons, and G. S. Pinnell (eds.), *Bridges to Literacy: Learning from Reading Recovery.* (pp. 119–147). Portsmouth, NH: Heinnemann.

Raphael, Taffy E., McMahon, Susan I., Goately, Virginia J., Bentley, Jessica L., Boyd, Fenice B., Pardo, Laura S., and

Woodman, Deborah A. (January 1992). "Research Directions: Literature and Discussion in the Reading Program." *Language Arts, 69,* 54–61.

Rosenblatt, Lousie. (1991). "Literature S.O.S.!" *Language Arts, 68,* 444-448.

Rosenblatt, Louise M. (1978). *The Readers, the Text, the Poem: The Trascactional Theory of Literary Work.* Carbondale, IL: Southern Illinois University Press.

Routman, Regie. (1991, 1994). *Invitations: Changing as Teachers and Learners K-12.* Portsmouth, NH: Heinemann.

Smith, Frank. (1988). *Understanding Reading.* (4th ed.) Hillsdale, NJ: Lawrence Erlbaum.

Strickland, Dorothy S. (1990). "A Model for Change: Framework for an Emerging Literacy Curriculum." In D. S. Strickland and L.M. Morrow (eds.), *Emerging Literacy: Young Children Learn to Read and Write* (pp. 135–146). Newark, DE: International Reading Association.

Taylor, Denny. (1993). *From the Child's Point of View.* Portsmouth, NH: Heinemann.

Teale, William H. and Sulzby, Elizabeth. (1990). "Emergent Literacy: New Perspesctives." In D.S. Strickland and L.M. Morrow (eds.), *Emerging Literacy: Young Children Learn to Read and Write* (pp. 1–15). Newark, DE: International Reading Association.

Vygotsky, Lev. (1979). *Mind in Society: The Development of Higher Psychological Processes.* Cambridge, MA: Harvard University Press.